Confessions
of a Full Time Mom

Publisher & Legal Information

Contents

To Mom.

Dear Full Time Mom,

Let me explain. Whether you're a married mom, a single mom, a new mom, a career mom, a stay at home mom, a working mom, a mom with toddlers, a mom with teens, a carpooling mom, an empty nester mom, you will always be a mom. Regardless of what season you are in, you will always be a Full Time Mom.

No matter the title you hold at home, at work, or in life, let's be completely honest, being a mom is hard! But, it's the MOST important job you will ever have. You were given this job because you are the right and perfect match for your child. God looked down, and out of all the women in the world he gave you this little being, or maybe more than one.

Wow! Soak in that for a little while...amazing isn't it?

So, yes, the days are long and the years go by fast...and easier said than done, right? My oldest daughter just turned 10 and I'm still figuring things out. However, I had 2 more girls, 18 months apart, and what I thought with my first child quickly changed each time I had another child. The point I am making is no child is the same, and the way you are with each one will not be the same either.

Give yourself a break because you are managing different personalities, needs, and feelings all at the same time you are managing your own needs, wants, and feelings. ***Gosh, this already sounds exhausting!*** Isn't that how being a mom is? Exhausting sometimes or maybe all the time, but also the most rewarding feeling ever.

When I started this project and started talking to mom after mom, I quickly realized each individual story was VERY different but the feelings and the wants were very similar. So, guess what??? Fourteen moms confessed specific moments that happened or that they experienced and got through. This book was written to remind you that you are NOT alone!!!

I hope this book brings you to a place where you can have an ah-ha moment, a crying moment, and a happy moment. I hope you realize how similar you are to many other women and moms out there. I hope you realize and learn that together is better than comparing and having mommy wars, which really do need to stop. We need to start listening and reaching out to each other, affirming we have a friend or twelve who will be there for one another through the happy times and through the dark times.

I pray these stories bring you hope and more importantly show you that we all go through moments which are joyful and at other times, not so much. I hope you can relate to one or more stories, and if you are going through the same moment, you can see how they coped and dealt through it. I hope you see that the mom like you is still standing, even stronger than before, and became an overcomer. May this book bless you and bring you hope beyond measures.

If you would like to be considered for the next edition, please email our team at: info@fulltimemom.org.

With Love and Light,

Francielle Daly

Confession #1 "Becoming Wonder Woman"
Elena Vela

"Good Morning Mommy" is how my bright toddler greets me in the morning with sunshine kisses and giggles.

I can smell the coffee brewing in the kitchen just waking my senses. I get up to take a perfect shower while The Best of the Beatles plays in the background on my speaker just preparing me for my day. I mean don't you just love upbeat happy music to start your day? I know I do.

I smooth on my styling mousse and my makeup seems to be on point. Looks like another fantastic day!

As I get out of the bathroom, my husband is finishing up fixing the bed, fluffing those decorative pillows. You know the ones you never use and you have to have a million of them because it makes your bed and room look super cute.

My toddler is all dressed and ready to go visit his grandma. He loves to have breakfast with her every morning with his daddy. It's the family bonding moment; you know they must have to build his childhood memories.

As I walk out, my kids are leaving to school, perfectly groomed and dressed, with their healthy lunches and homework done. "Bye mom, see you after work!"

"Bye, kids! We are having lasagna for tonight's dinner!" I replied.

I take a breath of fresh air. Affirmations are a great part of my life. Start your day with positive affirmations. It's going to be a great day! I am a winner! God is good!

My husband is pulling out of the garage so he can drive me to work. This is one of my favorite perks of being a stay at home dad during the day as he works nights. It's actually the perfect schedule. Dad has bonding time with our toddler doing what boys do, probably going to the mall to check out girls, getting car washes, doing some grocery shopping, maybe a visit to Toys R us, but definitely his favorite of going to baby gym time on Fridays.

I arrive at work with everyone saying their good mornings. I begin my day behind my desk checking my emails, and I hear a buzzing sound. Is that the fire alarm? It doesn't sound like a fire alarm….it sounds like a Wake-up Alarm set to my phone.

You know what's hard about having your phone set to an alarm, is that you can't slam it to snooze like you did back in the day on the clock alarms. So of course, I am not exactly fully awake. It seems that the morning alarm incorporated itself into my wonderful dream as a fire alarm.

What really woke me up was the empty baby bottle to my face. I believe my toddler has perfected his pitching arm. This kid might just give Jake Arrieta a run for his money. OK OK OK….I'M UP!

Sniffs what is that smell? Trust me it is NOT the smell of morning coffee. Oh! Well, let me tell you….my toddler seems to greet me so early by taking off his diaper full of poop and tossing it out of his crib.

What the...?! I thought only monkeys did that!!

I hope in to take a quick shower to wake me up. Ahhhh....awesome. No hot water. Seems that my kids beat me to shower time. Again.

Great. No time for blow drying my hair or getting that perfect brow done. Crazy mom hair it is.

Well, dad walked out to take the kids to school. So I guess I have to hurry.... fix the bed and get the toddler ready. Does anyone else have a toddler who does the ninja twist when you take off their diaper? Or maybe it's just mine. There goes 15 minutes just trying to get him changed, well at least all the kids are in school now.

Nope. Seems like one kid didn't hear his alarm, and is still in bed. Of course, everyone in my house has the mentality of "Every man for himself" they couldn't wake this kid up so he can get to school on time with them. Well, now I can expect a call from the Dean's office today, letting me know that my kid was late to school, you know because I need another adult reminding me of my lack of parenting.

I honestly feel like those phone calls are really telling me "Get your shit together lady, your kid is late to school because of you!" (I'm sure the phone calls are to let the parents know what time your kid arrives at school, but I usually take everything so personally. It's just how I'm wired).

So as my husband is installing the car seat in the truck, I'm football holding my toddler in one arm, as he's screaming and wiggling for me to put him down. (Probably so he can run and take his shoes off because he hates them), getting my stuff together in my purse in the other while holding my protein shake. Strap the boy in, and off to the train station. A ride to work on the train is 45 minutes, which means I'm 45 minutes late. Whoop-eeee.

While on the train I go through my calendar. I figure out what my deadlines are for the day or what's coming up during the week, maybe get my stuff done ahead of time, schedule doctor appointments, dental appointments, and parent/teacher conferences.

Oh crap! I forgot to sign permission slips for field trips and give it to the kids. I guess I have to email the teacher to admit my failed responsibility. Not even. Let me scan it to her email at least it will look like it was already done and I didn't forget.

Well, I got to work late. "Oh nice of you to come in, didn't think you were coming," said one co-worker.

*Gasp * Oh boo. No.

"I'm sorry I didn't realize you were the one who signs my paycheck or your name was on the door" I snapped. Now I have a little gloomy cloud of resting bitch face over me.
I settle in my desk preparing my work for the day.

I hope you weren't expecting a TV show sort of beginning to my confession, where you?

Well, that's just it. That is MY confession.

I can tell you most people think I do live a pretty cool, picture-perfect life. I mean, after all, I am a married mother of five plus three stepchildren, work a 9-5 job, run my own business (a children's clothing boutique), and balance my love, family, and social life.

Wow. That's a lot on your plate. I don't know how you do it all.

You know what's funny? I still feel that I'm not doing enough. I feel as though I'm wasting my time when I can add something else productive to my list. I feel like I have downtime in between things that I can manage to fill up. Maybe I can knock out one of my personal development books off my list each week (I have a list of over 100 books!), or maybe sign up for a business management course at my local college on the days that I close at my boutique.

Isn't crazy? I don't think so. Although, I'm not coming to you as a full time mom telling you all the terrors your one or two kids are going to put you through, and that everything will be ok in the end.

Oh no. Honey, no.

I am coming to you as a full time employee.
I am coming to you as a full time mother and wife.
I am coming to you as a full time business woman.
I am coming to you as a full time friend.

I will be the one who is going to cut it clean and feed it straight to you.
If you are easily offended, please don't bother to read on.

Wait. What how can you be a full time employee and a full time mother? That makes absolutely no sense.

Of course, it does. Last time I checked me and you have the same 24 hours in a day unless you are from Jupiter then you only have 9 hours. I just manage my time accordingly every single day. Just because your children are sleeping doesn't mean your mother title is off, or your duties are done for the day (I mean unless they are for you).

Honestly, having one or two even three kids is like vacation time to me. I am dead serious. I get so excited when my stepkids are with their mother, and a friend or my mother calls me to say they want to pick up one of my kids to go shopping or because they are lonely, or whatever the reason for that day is. Having one less child in the home to me is like the equivalent of sitting on a sunny beach drinking an icy cold margarita. Now before you crucify me and complain to me about how unfair I'm being and I get the "You don't know me, you can't compare," speech. I can't possibly be the only one who treats a kidless trip to Target like a mini vacation, where you want to go down every aisle knowing damn well you don't need to. Sipping your Starbucks. Alone. Enjoying your 1-2 hours of freedom.

Trust me I know exactly how hard things can be.

Before I got married to my current husband I was married for about 5 years. My marriage produced three children before ending it in February of 2006. My children were 4, 2 and 6 months old. I had to transform myself into a badass mom overnight considering I was far from it at that time in my life.

My "D" Day came that year when I made the decision to put my pride on the shelf. I promised myself I would never ask anyone for help. So in order to do that I had to change everything around me. I had to become mother and father, I took a new job offer, I eliminated friendships, and I even changed my name (not so much changed, but I now go by my middle name). I changed everything about me, it was a second chance at starting all over, and it was the best decision I have ever made.

Being a single mom of three was extremely tough at the time. I started a new 9-5 job, which required my utmost focus being the Executive Assistance for the main owner of our Firm. So I had to make sure that I had extremely reliable childcare for my children. I pulled my son from a private school and moved to the suburbs because they didn't have the resources available to me like a public school. I was also able to afford the daycare that was required for after hours without me having to inconvenience someone.

Every day I would rush out of work at exactly 5:01 pm to catch my train and make sure I was able to reach the daycare before it closed at 6 pm or else they would charge me $1 a minute per child. To go home and feed them dinner, get them showered, work on flashcards and other projects with them, get them to bed and prepare their stuff for the following day.

Once a week, we would have to go to the laundry mat around midnight to avoid the rush of people so I can finish my laundry faster. So here I am with my toddlers at the Laundromat at 12 or 1 am at night. Sometimes I would get home so late that my friends were coming out of the clubs and usually catch me outside unloading my laundry that they would always pull over and help, by this time it's about 2 am carrying in sleeping toddlers. Even though I was alone during this hard time, I sort of wasn't. Thank you God for my friends.

Each passing year, one child started to go to school, then another, alleviating my pockets from all day childcare. By this time I was in a relationship with my husband and had our first son.

A few years later, I married my husband. In 2011, I accepted 3 more children to my brood and welcoming our last in 2015, having a total of 8 children, 9 if you count my husband.

Do I really need to tell you that having a blended family is difficult?

The drama dealing with bipolar borderline schizophrenic humans and witnessing two grown adults fighting for the ridiculous things is appalling. I really do think that is probably another book on its own, you don't want to get me started on that topic.

But the only advice I may give on the subject is, don't make other people's problems your own if you have a full plate already. It adds to your stress level, as well as gray hairs on your head. I do not have any, but you should see my husband. Yikes.

So what can I tell you about my confession…?

Well, let me say this first.

I think people are so caught up with living up to society's expectations, that women are not doing things for themselves or their children. They do things based on what society expects of them. A square peg for a square hole if you will. Women have always been seen as the caretakers of the family. They stay at home caring for their husbands and children, cooking and cleaning, and making sure they keep their husbands happy if you know what I mean. *rolls eyes*

Just because you see a mom, who you think has their life together, with great hair, a killer body, a nice looking husband, and beautiful children driving the perfect car. Or maybe that single mom, who owns her own business, has her routine down to a T and her children are these geniuses in school.

Let me tell you something…… No one is perfect.

Perfection does not exist. People tend to judge others on the outcome of the visual, but never judge on the journey of a person who went through the struggles to get where they are at.

Did I lose you somewhere? Let me explain.

You know that mom with the great hair and a killer body that I just mentioned? Yea, she gets up at 4 am to prep herself to look amazing and hit the gym before everyone wakes up. That perfect car she drives with her husband is probably a result of pulling long hours at work.

That single mom who owns her own business that I just mentioned? She started planning that a year ago, you just didn't know. You didn't know about the sleepless nights she spent working tirelessly to make it perfect and spent the daytime for her children giving them extra attention to their curriculum and attending every teacher conference, or sit through all their science fairs.
But you didn't know all that, you just saw the outcome.

My point?

Your struggles will be hard, raising children, maybe finishing school, starting a new job, having an idea to start a business, and so on. Keep acting on those struggles one step at a time, moving forward and soon people will only see YOUR outcome. They will want to figure out how you did it.

All my struggles, till this day, are preparing me for challenges ahead. Every day you will encounter an obstacle, your perspective is what determines how you overcome it.

Raising children? Keep doing it, time will fly and you will notice the years pass as you see your children grow. Take pride and joy in every moment even though there might not be great times and you want to lock yourself in the closet from time to time. It happens. Trust me.

Dealing with Divorce? Remember life is short, and you don't have time for divorce....get it done and over with even if it means you are at a loss. (Trust me I know.) You have better things to do.

Hate your job? Find what interests you, what are you good at that your skills aren't being fully utilized, and start from there. You only stay at your job because you feel stuck. Remember, NO ONE owns you. Change is fearful, but I promise you when you deal with that fear head on, your life will change.

Need to lose weight? You can start by drinking water and changing your diet. Take up yoga, meditation, and don't forget to sleep!! Set yourself a small routine until it becomes a habit. Take one day at a time.

Well, you seem to have it together, how do you do it?

How do I do it? Well, I won't lie to you and say I never lose my shit. Trust me I do have those days. I am guilty for disappearing in my bathroom at least once a day.

But I do take it day by day. I try to spend as much time I can with my kids and husband, we do family involved things. When I run my business, my husband helps. I do have to give credit to where it is due. My husband is the biggest support system I have. We definitely bump heads on many things, but it never stopped him from giving his support.

So advice to you is stop living up to society's expectations. Do what needs to be done, and stop expecting things from the universe like it owes you. Don't worry about what others think or say about you, be your own kind of awesome. Learn to execute your goals even if they don't sound "Normal". What is labeled as normal now and days anyway?

So wrapping this up with my confession….

My confession is I learned to go against everything I was taught or told. I have learned that women are the Earth movers, the Earth stompers, the voice makers. If you have ideas, make them happen, they were given to you for a reason. God wouldn't put an idea or dream in your head if he didn't want you to act on it. You have 24 hours in a day, make the most of your hours. Learn to continuously develop yourself. Be the mom you wish to be. You are Wonder Women.

Confession #2 The Struggle is Real But God Always Provides!
Noreen Aguirre

Hello to all the mommies out there, I would like to share, my Confession with you as a mom, wife, author, pastor, radio host, and dental assistant. We may wear many hats and it may seem sometimes, there's no light at the end of the tunnel. But I'm here to share with you there is and even though the struggle is real the Lord always provides.

It's truly a blessing to be able to be called a Mom. I would like to dedicate this book, to my mom Chris Mercado, who passed away when I was 10 of Lupus leaving five children behind. To my siblings Nancy, Jose, Lechia, Frankie, and my angel that the Lord blessed us with and to help raise us all, my grandmother Rosa Mercado. Also to my five amazing children that the Lord blessed me with, Crystal Aguilar, Ashley Aguilar, Juventino Junior the 3rd Aguirre, Xzavion Aguirre, Nevaeh Aguirre, and my amazing husband Tino Aguirre Junior. Above all else giving Glory to my Lord and Savior!

Busy Busy Busy! Never enough time in the day to do it all.

My day pretty much starts off with a struggle every morning getting my kids up for school. As much as I would love to wake up before everyone in the house to read my Bible, pray, and spend some alone time with God. I start my day exhausted already. Thankfully my two oldest daughter's are on their own already but I still have my 15 year old and 9 year old who I have to get out the door and off to school.

Then, I am left with my three year old and our dog. Sometimes she is sleeping and letting the god out gives me enough time to have my prayer time.

As I'm fixing my bed and making sure everything's picked up and cleaned, I have worship music on in the background and this is my time to do praise and worship. Then I start, dinner! Yes, I start dinner usually at 8 a.m. and breakfast at the same time, before my daughter wakes up.

When she is finally up, I get her settled eating breakfast and rush down the stairs to put a load of laundry in. Since I have church service in my house, in the basement, I can never pass the Laundry room without praying so usually the basket of clothes goes down and my hands go up, to praise and worship God.

I start praying for everyone the Lord places in my heart. I pray for my family, my friends, and my YouTube supporters. Also, the people that reach out to me during the week to pray for them. When I'm done, I continue with the laundry then back upstairs to get ready for work and finish breakfast with my daughter.

After such a long day at work, I rush home before my husband leaves to work to make sure he has everything he needs, then help the kids with their homework.

After eating and spending some time together time to get them ready for bed. Then I run downstairs to the church area in my basement and I do my recordings for Facebook, YouTube, and Soar radio.com

When I'm done I come up to a pile of dishes staring at me, feeling so tired I just pray start talking to God asking him what would he like me to speak on next. Sometimes I feel frustrated when I come home to a dirty home after making sure I cleaned it before I left. I just stop to breathe, pray, and just thank God that I came home to a healthy family and that everyone's okay. The mess can wait, my sanity is so much more important.

Throughout my busy day the Lord is always talking to me and I'm always talking to him that's how I get strength and the patience to do what I can do for that day and that's how the Lord inspires me and gives me the messages to speak every week.

I work as a Dental Assistant 3 days a week and serve the Lord by ministering, praying, serving, and loving everyone who crosses my path. Through the messages I share every week, and through the books I Write they are for the glory of God. My first book is called, *"Godly Dreams Your Seat at the Table"*. Which was all inspired by God I share 40 prophetic dreams. It was through my prayers and guidance of the Lord and his strength I was able to publish that book. It was also my family that kept pushing me forward.

A little bit of my testimony

I had my first daughter at the age of 16 years old, with my first boyfriend at the time. We dated from elementary school for 8 years and had two children. At 21 years old I had my second child. Then I found out he wasn't faithful. Being responsible for my two daughters I decided to separate from him. I didn't want my daughters growing up thinking that it was ok for them to be treated this way. I raised my daughters on my own while going to school and working two jobs to pay for rent, a new car, food, and everything they needed. It definitely was a struggle, but through it all, I kept my faith in Jesus. He provided my every need. Through it all the Lord gave me the strength to do it all.

You see, when I broke up with my daughter's father I cried out to the Lord for about four hours, praying and worshiping him. I asked God for three things in my prayer. One was to help me forget my ex as if I had never been with him. Two ways to help me find somebody to marry that will love my children as if they were his own. And three, that the man I marry would be someone who will allow me to do all that God has called me to do. I got up from that prayer with so much strength from the Lord; boldness and confidence came over me. It was the strength I needed to raise my girls. I got up and never looked back.

I worked very hard to take care of my children and provide for them. I had two jobs. I would take care of an elderly lady in downtown Chicago, and I was a supervisor for a factory. For my first job, I would stay up all night, talking to the elderly lady, encouraging her, and massaging her feet. She was about 84 years old. She loved me, very sweet lady.

At the factory, I had to go around and make sure everyone had everything they needed to complete their job, but I did more than that. I got to know each person. I would talk to them and console them. I would inspire them to do better and do more with their life, encouraging them to go back to school praying for them.

Two to three days a week I would stay up all night with the elderly lady, go straight home, get my kids ready for school, drop them off, and then go to work at the factory. I remember almost every week rushing to drop my kids off at school. I would tell them, "time to hit the eject button," meaning they would have to get out of the car as fast as possible because I was running late for work. There were times that working two jobs and being a single mom was definitely a challenge but through it all the Lord gave me such strength, peace, joy, love, and patience. I was even able to accomplish my high school diploma. After dropping out of high school when I got pregnant with my first born.

There were definitely days that it was a struggle. With everything I had to do and pay for, some days we didn't even have money for milk. But the Lord always provided. I remember this like yesterday-- I was going through my closet, looking through some sweaters that were hung up, and dollar bills started flying at me as if somebody were tossing them to me. They were all singles. It was $13, enough to buy exactly what I needed until I got paid. Even though it was a struggle, through God's love, mercy, and favor, we did not lack anything.

I stood taking care of my children on my own for about five years before I married. My husband and I have been married now going on 16 years and have three more children together. He accepted my two daughters as if they were his own. My youngest daughter was only three years old at the time and my oldest was seven when I first met him. We quickly became really good friends. I could tell him anything. We talked for two years before we became boyfriend and girlfriend then about a year later he proposed to me. He's been truly a blessing, an angel here on Earth.

My oldest daughter is 26 now and my second daughter is 22. They still see their dad and do love him but they also have so much respect for my husband and love him as a father as well. All my children are very close. They respect each other and show each other so much love. I am so thankful for the type of people they have become.

The Lord has continued to be faithful and has fulfilled the third part of my prayer so long ago: I have been able to do all that God has called me to do and continue to do so with the support of my husband. I been a dental assistant for almost 16 years before the Lord place in my heart to stopped for 3 years to just focus on what the Lord has called me to do, which is taking care of my children and preaching the gospel around the world. So Godly Dreams Ministries was funded by my husband and God who is our number one provider. (I just returned back to work as a dental assistant part-time to help pay for everything that God has called me to do my books radio program and money to establish the church that God has called me to establish, for his glory.

I have been so blessed. Since completely, I have been able to write and publish a book, called *"Godly Dreams: Your Seat at the Table"*. On the night of its release, God gave me a vision for the second book, everything from what to write about, to the title and cover, pretty much everything! I am eager to continue and complete this vision

He has placed in my heart. I have also been fortunate enough to start a YouTube channel and radio show and have recently gotten my Pastoral License and have started services at home until I establish a church. I will never get tired of serving the Lord and reaching out to the multitude for the glory of God. Sometimes it feels like a lot, but then I remember everything He got me through in the past and I know that He will continue to provide.

So even though the struggle is real God always provides I pray that my confession of a full-time mom was a blessing to you please pick up a copy of my first book as well I know it will be a blessing to you as well and to everyone you share it with thank you so much for your love and support!

Author of **"Godly Dreams: Your Seat at the Table,"** is available through Amazon and Barnes & Noble, anywhere books are sold, I have an YouTube channel under my name please View and subscribe, and am the Host of Growing in Christ on SOARRADIO.com. God bless you!

And remember:

1 Corinthians 10:13 (Good News Translation) Every test that you have experienced is the kind that normally comes to people. But God keeps his promise, and he will not allow you to be tested beyond your power to remain firm; at the time you are put to the test, he will give you the strength to endure it, and so provide you with a way out.

Confession #3 They Deserve Better
Jessica Mondy

"Park. Play park. Play outside Mommy." My one and a half year old, pulls on my arm as I lay face down on the couch.

"Not today Baby." I don't even look up as I start another episode of Daniel Tiger. "Maybe tomorrow," I lie. Another beautiful day, wasted.

This lasts a few more hours. Until he starts putting his hand to his mouth, letting me know he is hungry. I roll myself off the couch to the kitchen. Turkey hot dog again today. As it heats in the microwave I fill a small bowl with frozen peas. They go into the microwave while I cut the hotdog and open an applesauce cup. He's had this for lunch every day this week, I remind myself. You're home all day. Where are the home-cooked meals? His plate of food feels heavy as I hand it to him. Something weighs down my chest—I take a deep breath but it doesn't go away.

"Thank you, Mama," he says as he takes the plate and turns back to the TV, back slouched, eyes glazed. I lie on the couch, cover my head with a blanket, and cry.

I've had a distant relationship with depression in the past, from insecurities in high school to the dreariness of November, but I had always avoided it. Over the years, the feelings of heaviness and hopelessness would come and go, but they never lasted. I could always shake them off. That is, until my second pregnancy.

I notice something is off immediately. I chalk it up to first-trimester exhaustion coupled with caring for a toddler. My son is turning one and the only date that works for his party is the one year anniversary of my previous miscarriage. I'm sure that's the reason why getting out of bed feels impossible and everything makes me weepy. This is obviously pregnancy hormones. This feeling of dread and emptiness is sure to pass.

Things do get easier once the second trimester comes around. My son is sleeping through the night and the second-trimester "energy boost" kicks in. The exhaustion subsides a little, but I still spend my days hiding on the couch, rotting my child's brain with Sesame Street and Thomas the Train. To be fair, he has learned most of his vocabulary from those shows, since I never read to him or coach him on colors, animals, shapes.

I even get myself a part-time job, teaching children to read (as if that's not ironic at all). I'm excited about the job and excel in the classroom. I am confident and calm and know exactly what to do. This pseudo-confidence gives me the false notion of being okay. Once distracted and busy, burdened with a purpose and instructions to follow, I can think straight and act decidedly. Outside the classroom is a different story. At home, I feel weighed down and sluggish, as if navigating the bottom of a lake. My paperwork falls behind and my supervisor is concerned. I have no energy for my son or the housework, despite my chipper attitude at work.

Ok, Jessica. We're going to the park, I tell myself. It's easy. Just put on shoes, put clothes on the baby, and we'll be there in 20 minutes. Yes, Good idea. I sit up. That's it. I can do this.

I look at my son sitting on the living room floor. He's long ignored the toys in front of him, fully engrossed in the animated trains.
It will be good to get him out of the house. Yep. It will be good for me too. Deep breath.

Why haven't I started moving? Stand up. My arms feel heavy. Stand up. My legs feel like nothing.

My son turns and looks at me. He smiles in a way that makes his eyes squint and holds his block out to me.

Look at me, taking my son to the park. I return his smile.

This is me, going to the park. He turns back to the TV and I lean back with my eyes closed, contemplating all the things I should be doing for him, but somehow can't. And I have no idea why.

I remember my job preparations caused me to hyperventilate. I rushed my son to his crib and then collapse in tears on the living room floor. I can't stop crying. I can't breathe. I desperately crawl to the shower to try to calm down. I sit down because my arms and legs go numb. It takes another twenty minutes with my knees tucked to my chest under the cold spray to be able to breathe normally.

I blame it on pregnancy hormones. I tell my doctor. He agrees. "As long as it doesn't happen every day." It's normal for pregnant women to cry. To cry on their way to work. To cry on their way home from work. To cry in the shower. To cry themselves to sleep. All this is normal.

It doesn't occur to me that I might have a problem until my 6-month appointment as I fill out the Prenatal Depression Screening Questionnaire (well, that makes sense). My answers to the questions do not surprise me. I know "things have been getting on top of me," "I have been so unhappy I have been crying," and that, "I have felt sad or miserable." What surprises me is how different they are compared to my previous pregnancy. What used to be "Hardly ever" and "Not at all" are now "Everyday" and "Most days." I was just as pregnant when I took the questionnaire then as I am now. I even spent my days chasing around a toddler. I was a nanny to a very active boy who was about the same age as my son now. What changed?

To make matters worse, I was a much better nanny than mother. We went to the park or library every day (even 8 months pregnant), the meals were balanced, and the TV was never on. Where is that girl? The girl I used to be. The girl who read stories and could run around the house and spend hours playing one on one. I try. I do. I pull out a puzzle or my son's Fisher Price farm and we play together on the floor. His eyes light up and his movements burst with energy as he shows me every piece with such excitement and joy. I last about 15 minutes before apologizing and grabbing the remote.

"No Mommy. Play. Play more Mommy."

"I'm sorry Baby. How about Daniel Tiger?"

"No. No Tiger. Play. Play more"

"No, let's cuddle. How about Dinosaur Train."

"Play Mommy. Play!"

"What about Curious George?"

". . . Ok."

I was a much better mother before I had kids. And now I have a second one on the way. That poor child, having to be stuck with me as a mother.

I do what I can to change. I tell myself things like, I deserve to be happy, I can do this, and Jesus loves me, but the words are meaningless.

"Meaningless."

Now there's a word I can understand. It's one of the few words that make sense, along with "failure" and "worthless."

I know my son deserves better. My unborn son deserves better. They deserve a mother who plays with them, and reads to them, and is involved in their lives beyond keeping them alive. My husband deserves a better wife. That poor honorable man. He deserves a medal after this. He is so patient with me. He doesn't ask me what I've done all day. He doesn't chastise me for doing anything. He is much more gracious to me than I am with myself- than I am with him. He comes home to a ruined house and a closed off, exhausted wife who wants nothing to do with him beyond asking him to change diapers. God, they deserve so much better.

I need to leave. They deserve better than me, a better caretaker, and a better partner. They aren't going to find someone better if I am still around. So I will run away, make myself disappear. Not because I'm searching for my own happiness, but because I'm hoping to bring them theirs. Once my son is born, I'll wait a few months, and then do what I can to get as far away as I can. Our friends and family will flock to my husband and the boys, overflowing with sympathy, and that will get them by until they can find their "Someone Better." The thought of never seeing my son again breaks my heart, but the thought of him being stuck with no one but me breaks it even more.

And so the months go on.

Some days are better than others. Occasionally the dishes get done and laundry put away. I'm still my son's favorite person despite my obvious failings. The more I try to accomplish around the house, the more my personality deteriorates. I snap. I yell. I make my son cry over spilled juice. My husband, who works all day and then comes home to a filthy hormonal mess, gets nothing but criticism and disrespect.

When I try keeping my cool and being patient and calm, it takes all of my mental energy to do so. Nothing is left over for, well, anything else. No work, no play, no joy. I am either a ticking time bomb or an empty shell. There is no in between. Just a few more months, I tell myself.

"Jessica, you are made in the image of God. You are His masterpiece. You have talents and dreams and you have been put on this Earth to do good works."

Wow, that Jessica sounds amazing. I wonder who she is. Maybe I knew her at one point, but not anymore. That Jessica is gone.

By now I have spoken to another doctor about the questionnaire and she told me I needed to make an appointment with the psychiatrist. Oh great, I thought, that means drugs. I was uncomfortable with antidepressants because of the stigma surrounding them and the stories I've heard of their failures. Years of uncertainty and uncomfortable side effects, having to try more and more medications in higher and higher doses in order to find one that worked. That coupled with the fact of my inherent failure-as-a-human-being had me convinced I could never be cured.

My son is screaming. It's late. Bedtime. It's been a long day. The dishes and dirty living room floor are mocking me and weighing down my chest. Every time I try to step away, to calm down, to take a breath-my son is there. Needing something, wanting something; not always moving, always touching, always making noise. I feel the strings in my mind pull so tightly they could snap. I flex and curl my fingers to keep them from twitching. I hold my breath to keep from shouting. I hear the door. Oh, thank God Josh is home. I hand him a screaming toddler and bury myself under the covers in the dark.

Now it should be noted that Josh hardly ever puts my son down to bed. I've done it, nearly every night, for over a year and a half. My son was not having it.

"Mommy. Want Mommy. Want Mommy. Want Mommy. Mommy! Mommy! Mommy!!"

Hearing his tear-soaked cries in the dark broke the remains of a shattered heart. How could I leave him? How could I do that to him? It made me angry. It's not right. It's not fair. How can he not understand what a failure I am? Why doesn't he understand that he deserves better? It's obvious he doesn't care what's best because he only wants me. It broke my heart. My tears were quieter, but lasted much longer, than his.

In my desperation, I reach out to, of all places, an online parenting community. I need to express myself in anonymity and expect to be more or less ignored. But something crazy happens. People notice. They respond. They tell me how much my son needs me and that I am, in fact, a good mother, the best mother, for my boys. It's something I can conceptually agree with. But "knowing" I am the best mother for my boys and "believing" it is two entirely separate things. While I'm not convinced, reading the pleas of internet strangers plants the idea in my head that it might be true. Their words give me hope, something I had forgotten the taste of.

They convince me to get help. Starting with telling my husband exactly how I feel. He knew about the problem, but I very carefully hid how severe it had gotten (for surely if he knew of my plan he would have ruined everything). Second, I scheduled a psychiatric appointment. I hung up 2 or 3 times before getting through the menu to a receptionist. Afterward I cried. I cried because I was tired of feeling this way. I cried because the hope that I might get better was too exhausting and painful to bear.

But I went. I spoke. I listened. I was given a prescription. I took that prescription. And I rejoiced.

Is this how normal human beings feel? Every day!?
It had been so long, I had forgotten what it felt to be. To exist. I felt like a genuine person for the first time in far too long. Looking back now, I don't know why I waited. When I consider the weeks and months my son was without an active, involved mother I hate that I waited.

I was lucky that my first round of medication worked wonders; some people do struggle with what prescriptions to take and what dose. But there is now a genetic test than can be done to determine which drugs will interact most favorably with your body. Even if it had taken months of trial and error, my recovery would have been worth it.

My younger son is now a year old and I can't imagine being anywhere else but here, playing with and guiding and loving my two boys. I'm not perfect. I still struggle. But I can proudly say that I am here for them, both physically and emotionally. I didn't get here on my own: I have God, my husband, and Zoloft to thank for that. The journey was long and dark, but the destination is more than worth it.

If you think you're going through something similar: GET HELP NOW. Even if it's just reaching out to a trusted friend or family member, do something. Tell someone. Check out the websites and hotlines (available 24/7) listed below. But neither I nor the internet can diagnose mental illness. Go to a doctor. Be honest. If the first doctor blows you off, find another one. Keep going back until you get what you need: be it coping mechanisms, therapy, or medication. Don't be afraid. Or rather, act despite the fear. You CAN overcome, but you can't do it alone. Your family deserves a real you. You deserve to feel real again. God and I believe you can do it.

National Hopeline Network: 1-800-SUICIDE (784-2433)
https://hopeline.com/

National Suicide Prevention Lifeline: 1-800-273-TALK (8255)
https://suicidepreventionlifeline.org/

Substance Abuse and Mental Health Services Administration (SAMHSA): 1-800-662-HELP (4357)

Confession #4 Birthing Is Ageless
Carol Wachniak

The early morning sun was shining through the open window of our bathroom. In my hand was an at home pregnancy test, the positive results staring me in the face. I redid the test and checked it 4 times, still getting the same results. "I'm going to be 44 in April!" Imagine, already having seven children and then you discover that magical number eight was on the way.

Overwhelmed, my mind began to race, feeling like my finger was in the electrical socket, unable to comprehend an explosion of emotions. A rainbow of super-charged colors went from my brain to my stomach. Knots swelled up inside. Fears, insecurity, and doubt began running through me. Another baby! I mean, I thought our family was complete. It wasn't a question of whether or not I wanted this child, but could I physically do this again? Pregnancy and labor? Could we, as a family, get by and care for another child when there are seven older ones?

I was in the doctor's office when I had a breakdown moment. How many of you have had one? I'm crying profusely, repeating, I don't know if I can do this. I don't know. I don't know." Dr. White said, "This baby is going to be such a blessing. You are so blessed, and you're having this baby for a reason." I, a doula, needed the wisdom of another professional. He had a vision and understanding of where I was in this birth process that was bigger than I could see for myself.

I had to ask myself some serious questions. Were the criticisms and judgments I was hearing from other people or myself? Were these criticisms and judgments really true? The baby wasn't the problem, it was my thoughts. It was the conversation going on in my head. What I really needed was perspective.

A friend said, "I'll pray for acceptance for you." Wow. That woke me up.

Am I willing? Willing to grow? Willing to trust God's wisdom or my own? Am I willing to look honestly at myself? Was I looking at what I really needed to be looking at, that is, my yearnings? Yearnings are foundational: they run in the conversations of our inner spirit. Everyone has them and when you're aware of them, they are the guiding light to what you're creating or experiencing.

Here are a few to help you understand:
to be safe and secure;
to love;
to be loved, wanted, and valued;
to connect to something bigger than ourselves;
to fulfill your full potential and purpose;
to create, to contribute;
to feel "felt", seen and heard;
to learn to grow and develop
to know God.

These yearnings play a key role in our creating and birthing experiences. When I stilled myself enough to begin to listen from the inside of my heart, I could see how I wanted to be safe and secure. My first emotional response the situations was fear. Imagining a loss of security for myself and my family hit me between the eyes. But slowly I began to see. I was only looking at the facts, which enlarged my emotions, fears, and insecurities. Once I started looking at the big picture, I began to see a little flicker of hope, a small ember of light shining at the end of the dark tunnel. Even though I didn't know how everything was going to work out, I had to make a choice. I could believe the thoughts of doom and gloom or I could begin to connect to something bigger than myself.

My biggest concern at that time was obviously being able to provide for our children, financially, physically, and emotionally. Struggling with my sense of worthiness, confidence in my abilities was wavering. I questioned if I'd be able to give my children all they needed. I started to read Proverbs 31: 10-31 and I realized there's something going on here, which this was going to take me, my life, and my business to another level.

"She provides food for her family... She has no fear for her household... She can laugh at the days to come"

A gentle breeze of peaceful knowingness swept across my mind. My worthiness issues were being addressed. The feelings of "I am loved, wanted and valued" began to germinate and grow. The awareness that this new baby is only coming to contribute, to love, be loved, wanted, and valued. Was I willing to learn to let go, to grow, and develop myself? The picture I had in my mind shifted. This new baby wasn't going to disrupt our lives and safety. This baby was here for a reason: to help me, if I was willing, is part of a new creation. This new life is here to contribute to humanity and to fulfill our shared potential and purpose. This very small seed of faith in my heart began to beat, right along with hers.

Thump thump. Thump thump.

I knew somehow we'd get by if I stayed in the present moment, not running into the painful contractions of the future or the painful contractions of the past, those painful, trying times of change and transition, that's where fear and loss of security labored in my mind. I started to feel lighter and more refreshed. Why? Because my thoughts and beliefs had now begun to change. Since having our 8th child, some things happened in our life that was completely unexpected, especially in my business, which made life more difficult. But even in our hardest and most difficult moments, when we didn't think we could get by, we discovered that this baby number eight was one of our biggest blessings. I am so grateful for my beautiful, incredible daughter, as well as my seven other amazing children.

How many other moms or parents are in an overwhelmed state? I can share my experience with them, with you, because I've been there and I've had those feelings. I can be present, anchored, and real with you just as I am with myself. That's why I am writing this chapter, here and now, to share my experiences, my insights, and my hope. The Golden Thread of Truth runs from one heart to another. Wisdom and Birthing skill sets are being transferred over. When I went to see Dr. White, he wasn't just my physician; he was a confidant, a dear friend, and one of my mentors. His 45 years of Birth experience gave him a solid credibility and authority to transfer his skill sets to me, an expectant mother who needed to find the way through. After 37 years of my own living and Birthing experiences as a doula, I know I'm here for a greater purpose. I'm here to inspire others, like you, when they're in their contractions of life. I'm a voice for others, letting them know, just like Dr. White envisioned for me, that it's going to be okay.

"This will become one of your greatest blessings."

Whether you're on your first child or eighth, I am here to help you see the magic of the present day moments, to let go of the fear and the doubt that comes with parenting, and rise to the occasion of your greatness as a parent. As I stand here in front of you I feel like I'm being blessed by you, because you're going to make the most amazing parent in the world. I know that because I believe in you, just as others have believed in me.

Bio: Wife and Mother of eight, grandmother to twelve. Philanthropist, Legacy Leader, CEO of Genesis 1 Management LLC Social Enterprise, Founder of the Educational Foundation for the Children of Fiji 501c3, Inspirational Speaker, Radio Show Host, Professional Doula. I wrote a book, check it out. *"The Original Birth Whisperer: Life Lessons of a Doula."*

Confession #5 The Nest
Whitni Hey

I was the youngest of three children. Soon after I was born my mother divorced my dad and became solely responsible for supporting us. We moved often, which meant changing schools and always leaving friends behind. Hence, my brother and sister were my best, most stable and encouraging confidants. Before graduating high school I had gone to 13 different schools so consequently, this influenced the reason for my planting such deep roots here in our home of 38 years.

When asked what I wanted to be when I grew up, my answer was to be an "actress and singer" but never without adding that I also had to be, "A lady just like my mother". She was a strong, loving, and capable influence. Yet, there were times when I remember her coming home and being so tired that she would just collapse. I realize now what she sacrificed and how difficult that it must have been to raise us while working full time. I never heard her complain but instead, she told us how thankful she was for our lives. It's her cheerful, determined, positive, attitude that I strive to live out even now.

When I was 13 years old, my mother married a minister in Chicago and we ended up as a blended family with five teenagers. It wasn't much like the Brady Bunch but I was happy to see my mother's joy. Soon my stepfather was transferred to a small town church about 100 miles away from the city. I wasn't very excited to move again, but this change in my life is one for which I will be forever grateful.

I attended a college near Chicago and decided to come home for a Thanksgiving break after a stressful college semester
to visit my family and restore. It was then that I encountered my future husband and fell madly in love. Time was magical with him: that first night we gazed at the stars speaking of dreams and philosophy and bonded with a spiritual communion. I knew that incredible night that I would marry him. Our first date was on December 5 and spent almost every day following together. On December 14 he asked me to marry him and we were married March 21, 1981...the 1st day of spring.

Our marriage has been a happy one. We share many interests like making music, traveling, and nature. At first, it was just us growing and learning about one another for 2 years before our first child was born. We both knew that eventually we wanted to start a family, but I always imagined myself with a career in musical theater beforehand. Those dreams quickly took a backseat once I found out I was pregnant. I became immersed in the honor of being able to grow a life inside of me.

I was such a happy pregnant person. I loved being the vehicle for God's greatest miracle. To think that I could do something so profound was beyond all deserving and the greatest privilege. To be part of His masterpiece was sacred and inspiring and I was humbled. She was mine and we shared a personal relationship unlike any other and I couldn't dream of doing anything more important! I marveled at all of the stages of growth and felt more complete than ever before; feeling as if I was filled with heaven. There was even a bit of sadness as I drew close to delivery. I was excited to meet my new little friend but I didn't want the intimacy to end. I knew she was perfectly safe with everything she needed inside me.

On August 17, 1983, I delivered our first child. She was a beautiful baby girl who we named Genesis. It was a new beginning of life for her and for us. Labor lasted 36 hours but I felt reverence and an almost mystical familiarity with the experience. I was one with God and with all of the mothers that ever were. The timelessness and communion that I felt being able to participate in this incredible act were immense. I was focused and centered and felt in unison with my body and all that was happening to it. There was calm and peace that settled over me as I relaxed into the closeness of a heaven on Earth. I felt a spiritual lifting that I had never felt before as I held the precious miracle in my arms for the first time. There was no greater love than this.

I remember wondering how having this child would change the relationship that I had with my husband. I treasured those times when it was just the two of us and pondered what bringing another into our world would do to the relationship. What I found was that this life that we helped create together brought us a deeper connection and respect. Genesis became my constant companion and I didn't feel like I needed anything else other than my endearing little family. Other ideas of what a "successful" woman meant for me melted away. I realized my unparalleled value as I gazed into my baby's eyes.

There was a purpose in each day and it meant being the best mother and wife that I could be. In 1986 and 1989 our little family was blessed with the additions of two additional blessings...this time both were sons; James III and Andrew. James III was amazing and precious and splendidly unique. And, Andrew was an unexpected joyful and beautiful light who filled a very special place that no one else could ever occupy. It's like the spokes of a wheel; the unit as whole gains strength from each other's support and if one is removed, there is weakness and instability. We all had our place.

I was lucky enough to be a stay-at-home mother and my husband was very encouraging and excited about me being able to be there for the kids. I strived to do a perfect job taking care of the kids and in making our home life wonderful because he worked hard to support us. Those years of watching the kids growing up on our 12 acres were pure, simple delight. They were the messengers of what God's love is all about.

They were the days of music, make believe, and blanket forts covering the living room. At night we would read wonderful books together snuggled on the couch. We'd pass time outside imagining fantastic scenarios, discovering the incredible wealth of nature, and passionately creating projects. They were precious years and I felt joy unequaled. Other than doing the "kid things," I was not involved much with extraneous commitments. I loved being a mom.

We were integrated into each other's lives and we shared a love without condition. I felt an urgency to hold onto time and freeze it. The busyness of life was so busy at times that I would occasionally call the kids off from school to go walking in sparkling winter snow or to take a picnic in the woods to look for wildflowers. We loved observing the beautiful diversity of this glorious world. I also enjoyed getting to know their friends on school field trips. We had many youngsters around our home and I was "Mom" to a lot of special people along the way. Home was a place they could express themselves without judgment and even now we maintain friendships. It's so important to teach kindness, tolerance, and compassion and I am rich because of our lives intertwining. However, as time flew by, I realized there was nothing I could do to alter the ticking of the clock.

The school years went by in the blink of an eye. There was much activity and many marvelous things happening. I was involved with parent/teacher committees, dances, special events, and room help. There were piano lessons, track, wrestling, baseball, soccer, basketball, football, cheerleading, gymnastics, plays, and musicals. With everything that they wanted to do we were there encouraging them on the sidelines. Those were fabulous days. Before long though, graduation had come and gone and it was time for them to leave the nest.

Even though we knew that we would miss them, we were thrilled that all three of our kids were able to attend college. It was what we dreamed and hoped for our kids as they transitioned into healthy adults. We were excited knowing that they'd be able to learn and grow independently discovering themselves away from home. When dropping off each one, I would show a proud smile as we waved goodbye pulling away from the curb but, inside my heart felt like it was breaking. I came to the realization that things were evolving and that I needed to find my identity again as they were establishing their own as individuals. Just as it was always hard to have summer come to end; it signified another important milestone of time.

Sometimes I'd go into their rooms and reminisce while weeping on the bed. I remembered all the nights tucking them in and singing and talking and then when they were adolescents, just listening was enough. I was having a hard time letting go of a blessed time that I cherished so deeply. They were my whole world and I felt them slipping away. I would have to figure out who I was separate from them and what I would do next. Those were tough questions and I didn't have the answers.

At the beginning of this new phase, I was uncertain what the relationship would be between my husband and I now that the kids had moved out. We needed to re-figure what "we" were. Much of "us" had included our kids. We had both evolved and there was a need to get reacquainted in a sense. We are certainly lucky to have made it work all these years. I have a great appreciation for all we built together. Every experience along the way helped create our story and our joined perspective has been the beautiful guide and filter.

I used to feel like I needed to validate and defend myself as a stay-at-home mom when I heard the question, "What do you do?" I came from a background surrounded by strong, independent, working women and thought that it was what my future dictated. Having a successful career was an expectation I had for myself and all that I knew being raised by a single, competent mother. In time though, I found liberation with self-examination and clarity in my own personal journey. The job of homemaker and mother is what I chose to do.

It is important for mothers to understand that there is no "right" way to raising kids. There is no specific recipe nor is it a competition as each family dynamic is unique. We're bombarded with the "do's" and the "don'ts" and "proper" guidelines of what will make the "perfect" parent. There are those who will say what you are doing is too much and others that it's not enough. The best thing to do is to be true to yourself and to your children. When fearing repercussions or a possible mistake, children become smothered under a canopy of protection or occupied with just too much distraction. The formal classroom and paid for lessons are great but in the end pursuing harmony and remembering that we are the first teachers who will influence their fragile spirit, expression, and confidence is essential.

Finally, I've come to a place where I can rearrange the rooms and change things in the house. It was difficult for quite a while since familiarity was a sweet comfort. I had altered little from the time our children were small but I find the leap was cathartic and cleansing. I'm in a different chapter with my grown kids, who I see now as affectionate, considerate, loving adults. I am proud of what I see. I'm embracing this time and have discovered rewarding ways to engage my other interests. There is more time to do things with my dear husband such as making and recording music together, painting, and traveling to incredible, undiscovered places. I am also writing and finishing the process of getting a college degree. Besides that, I have other new little ones to make room for as the blessings of grandchildren start filling our lives. Each part of my life has offered something amazing and I look forward rather than back with positive optimism and excitement for what God has prepared for me next.

As I age and time accelerates, there is more urgency in living fully. I realize that aging is a privilege denied to many and time's transience urges me to make a difference and leave behind a worthy legacy. Life is not about finding something "out there" but seeing the extraordinary in the ordinary moments and celebrating along the way. As caretakers of our children and the majestic Earth, we can determine a bountiful goodness that creates a ripple effect of solidarity. There is integrity expressed in each living thing: in the animals, plants, bugs, and all that encompasses this incredible planet....a beautiful dance that is everlasting and so very precious.

The passage of time is a wise reminder to slow down. Life is a powerful process of letting go from the moment we are born. First from the womb and then every step after that is a measure of release ending eventually with our own life. I am part of a chronicle of splendid entanglement having the knowledge that I'm connected to an ancient web of being. Life embodies an amazing process of life, death, and regeneration. This world is a magical place if you meander leisurely using the potential of all your senses. Breathe deep, slow down, and look around holding dear ones near. Time waits for no one. When the kids were growing up, I felt like time was the enemy. Now he feels like an old friend as I watch the beautiful circle unfold. I feel an enchanted rapture in growing older as I continue to experience countless wonders with an appreciative and overflowing heart. The future excites me as I look at all the life that continues to abound with the births of our new babies and I celebrate the love that is exceeding as we breathe together in a collective breath.

Confession #6 Defining Mom
Stephanie Beeby

What does it mean to be a mom? Who defines this pivotal role that is crucial to existence? For years, I was the over-achieving, go-getter, single woman, an entrepreneur with a heart. I had ideas and I ran with them. There wasn't ever a challenge I couldn't face or excel in. That is until I became a mom. I thought I knew what it meant to be a mother. I thought I knew what I was getting myself into when I had my son, but it was as if a whole new world opened to me that I didn't even know existed. Don't get me wrong, I had been around kids and I was an incredible aunt. I had worked with ADHD, ADD, and autistic kids in high school as well as college, but nothing prepared me for being a mom. It's something you can't really prepare for until you are fully immersed in all the aspects of what it truly means. I connect it to trying to teach someone to swim in the ocean when they have never seen water.

While I was trying to discover the meaning of being a mom, I looked back at my lineage. My maternal grandmother had never gotten a driver's license. My grandfather didn't think she needed one. Her sole role was "stay at home mom and wife," and that is what she did best. She was the good Christian wife, who put her husband first and definitely her kids. She passed at 76 and never had the opportunity to experience the adventure and independence that driving a car can bring. This made her dependent on others all of her life. For this, she was both grateful and resentful.

Then there is my paternal grandmother, Nan. She straddled the role of entertaining, independent woman and young mother and wife. She married at 16 in England and came over to the States with my grandfather whom she had met in WWII. They had kids immediately and 10 years later, when the relationship deteriorated, she had the courage to leave him.

She did get married again, this time with a different focus, not for love as much for stability. She needed a good father figure for her two sons. She found him and remarried in her 30's, then had another son. Her focus was still to "please" her man, but she held her own stance in the world. She was independent, but also selective. As I look at both of these women's influence in my life, I see I definitely lean towards the example of my paternal grandmother: forging my own path, being clear about what I want, and defining the expectations of the roles husband and wife.

Now, let's look at my own mother. She wanted to go to college right out of high school, but the nearest one was miles away. Since she didn't have a driver's license, she wasn't able to figure out transportation. She consequently received training, obtained her driver's license, secured a job, and then met my dad and got married at 19. For the first six years of my life, she was her mother's daughter--dutiful, subservient, always putting her needs last.

Then the divorce happened. It broke the pattern of the past and she showed her true colors of courage and fortitude. She went back to school and got an Associate's degree, got herself a better real estate job, and created a successful career. She became the person she was raising me to be: strong, confident, goal-oriented, and kind. She taught me how looks fade and that I need to ensure there is something deeper to fall back on.

In summary, the biggest lessons of my feminine line include:
  Be Strong;
  Be Resilient;
  Leave when you can't be yourself;
  Know what is important to you;
  Make sure you can take care of yourself no matter what;
  There is power in dreams, even if they don't all come true.

Even after contemplating all the accomplishments and strengths of my familial role models, the concept of motherhood continues to elude me. The landscape of being a mother has transformed since even my mom's era. We are challenged to deal with more information, more knowledge, more technology, and more awareness than ever before. We are faced with listening to our intuition all while so-called-experts share differing opinions on how to properly care for our children. Attempting to raise our kids in the Information and Internet age comes with ease on some fronts and a huge responsibility on others. Balancing the multitude of pressures we face as we navigate these undiscovered territories require fortitude, stamina, and a willingness to grow. Motherhood comes with a pre-requisite of continual growth, the openness to expand, and the humbleness to ask for more help than ever before.

When my son was first born I felt at a complete and total loss. Thank goodness I still had my career. It was the only area of my life that I felt I excelled in and gave me the confidence I needed as a new mom. I remember the first mommy-and-me meeting that I attended. We were all still pregnant at the time and all the moms told me they were going to leave their work to become full-time mom-only types once the baby was born. It freaked me out. I had none of those urges. I couldn't imagine not having my calling in life. My career is aligned with my truest gifts and to give that up, just for becoming a mom, felt like a loss I wasn't willing to entertain. I knew I was doing my work in the world and I needed to know that was not going to change by having a child.

In the car, I cried all the way home. I sat in meditation and connected with this not-yet-born soul in my womb and asked him, "Did you come here to keep me from doing my work?" And I heard, "No mom, we are different. We will work together to do your work," and that is when I knew that my path of becoming a mom was unique for me. It was different from the other moms at mommy-and-me and different from my mother and grandmothers. It is unique for each and every one of us who attempt this marvelous journey.

We all have these magnificent souls coming through us and we share lessons, share rewards, and share resources. There is a reason they chose us and us them. I was hit with the deep realization that "mother" isn't so much a noun as it is a verb. It is something we define through our actions. It also requires us to challenge some of the outdated concepts that require us to be a full-time mom-only in order for us to take this role seriously. Even after my son was born, I still didn't have a clear definition of the idea.

I decided to approach this as I do everything, by breaking it down into what end results I wanted. As with my intuitive business coaching, it is imperative that you know your destination in order to determine the best path to get there. I looked at the concepts and definitions of "mother" that surrounded me, from mommy meet-ups to my family history. I then worked to define the key aspects of motherhood as I wanted it to be, not what others said it was.

The principles I chose to focus on are:
Teach compassion, by being compassionate and giving;
Share unconditional love, always and without exception;
Leave space for downtime, quiet time, and reflection - recharging is a part of life;
Play- build the imagination, laughter is important;
Honesty is safety- being truthful in action and speech;
Build community- relationships are key to life;
Own my stuff- —take ownership of my emotional states, mindset, and feelings.

The list I created through this process leads me to now examine how I was living my own life. Was I modeling all of these? Would my son be able to see these concepts in my words and actions? A wise woman once taught me that you can always train for skill, but it takes more to build character. For me, it was about modeling; being and reflecting the most important lessons that I felt called to instill in my son.

In truth, I felt I was doing a pretty good job. Where I needed to stretch myself the most was in the play component, but I was sure my son could definitely be the teacher in this aspect. I also needed to continue to check my language and actions and ensure that I wasn't over-projecting my state of being onto my son. It's funny how much you become aware of when you start to take note of your language pattern. Consider the statements: "You are driving me crazy right now," or, "the choices you are making right now aren't making mommy happy." Both of these statements weren't modeling what I wanted to convey. Once I realized this, I shifted my language. I chose, "Please use your inside voice, mommy has to focus right now," and, "your choices are not setting you up for what you want. What can you choose now to allow you to choose wisely?" Believe me, this was not a practice that changed overnight. It continues to take daily focus and awareness. I noticed how much easier it is when I have had enough sleep!

Pressure comes with the territory as a mother, and especially for a mother and empathy. The raw vulnerability can be overwhelming at times. I have had to learn an entirely new level of self-care than ever before. This goes beyond the regularly scheduled pedicures and massages, though I would definitely like more of these. It comes down to sacred me time: time to write, journal, read, reflect, pause. It is a time for hearing my own voice and catching up on no-responsibility recharge time. I needed to slow down and allow my own dreams to become apparent once again. This was one of those never ending tasks that I thought I had no space for during the first 3 years of my son's life. This is the area that has stretched me the most since becoming a mother.

A huge part of the expansion also centers on the level of love we hold for our child, which extends far beyond what we can ever truly experience for ourselves. Or perhaps, it is the jumping off point to experiencing more love, more joy, and more pleasure. If we only knew how to harness the same presence we hold for our kids and give it to ourselves.

Motherhood takes us through this metamorphosis from having to only care for ourselves to completely giving ourselves over to another human being, especially if you are breastfeeding or the only parent who gets up in middle of the night. Given I was one of those moms who couldn't pump successfully and breastfed exclusively; it was quite a challenge juggling the lack of sleep for as long as I did. Only 3-hours at a time for over 2-years--it was what I imagine training for some special ops military team would be like but with way less excitement!

Healthy self-sacrifice requires a shift of consciousness. I started as the "do everything for others" kind of mom, and slowly became the "self-loving, self-caring" kind. I found that the more I cared for myself, those around me were more cared for as well. We can only fill others up from a cup that is full. Ensuring that we think about our own desires, needs, and wants is essential to our long-term success as a mom or parent. If we don't, then I can see how it becomes easy to get resentful of the role and just shut down, which serves no one. As I honor the wisdom of the mothers before me, I recognize how far we have come and how the role of the woman/mother continues to evolve. I see how the self-sacrificial energy is still present, but with the awareness that I can choose differently. I can choose to demonstrate self-love, self-care, and self-compassion. I can pass these down to my own child through my choices and actions.

I choose to model downtime with meditation and yoga. I model health with outdoor hikes and working with my personal trainer. I choose to demonstrate success by dedicating my efforts on projects that financially and emotionally align with who I am. I choose to demonstrate the power of learning by listening to books on tape while in the car and reading hardcover books on my lazy Sunday afternoons.

Reflecting on it all, I am still unsure of the kind of mother I am becoming, but I honor the wisdom of the unknown and the luxury to even reflect on this question. Defining the term "mom" for yourself is the key to ensuring you can stand in the mirror and be proud of who you are becoming. Motherhood continues to be the most fulfilling and stretching experience of my existence. I trust my son is my greatest teacher and I am his as well. What a different perspective to think that our roles are not set in stone but have the power to evolve, just as we do.

Confession #7 The Skinny on Motherhood
Genesis Hey Krick

Tap Tap Tap! I begrudgingly open my eyes as I am woken up from a dead sleep. As my blurred vision starts to come into focus, the silhouette of a little person becomes clear. My five year old is, yet again, at my bedside "wanting mommy." This is an ongoing habit for him. A rather exhausting habit if I do say so myself. I push myself up to look directly into his little face and ask him, as I have countless times before, "What's wrong honey?" He always has the same answer:"I'm scared. "But what are you scared of, Sweetie?" He is not sure but he wants to be close to me. I can't help but feel frustrated even though I know he only wants care and comfort. This frustration is normal for a mommy, right?

Motherhood is hard. I sometimes find myself so physically and mentally exhausted; it feels impossible to move forward with the day. I have to admit there are days where all I want to do is cuddle up in a cozy blanket and lay in my warm bed. The days when I could completely relax and have no worries are long gone unless of course, my husband lets me have a spa day! The reality of it is, when we become mothers we naturally worry more, sleep less, take care of ourselves less, and eat less. We don't have as much time for basic things, such as shower, read, workout, etc. It is not because we don't want to do these things but we are spending all our time taking care of someone else's needs. While it is important for us to meet all of our children's needs, it is equally important for us to take care of ourselves. Easier said than done.

On top of the responsibilities and inherent stress that come with motherhood, I face another challenge. In 6th grade, I was diagnosed with an autoimmune disease by the name of Hashimoto's Disease, which can cause some pretty nasty side effects.

Some of them include:
  -weight gain
  -fatigue
  -paleness or puffiness of the face
  -joint and muscle pain
  -constipation
  -inability to get warm
  -difficulty getting pregnant
  -joint and muscle pain
  -hair loss or thinning, brittle hair
  -irregular or heavy menstrual periods
  -depression
  -slowed heart rate

Isn't that fun! Everything you wouldn't want as a woman and busy mother, right? I want you to know some of my struggles to let you know you are not alone. We all have them. They are different, but we all have setbacks keeping us from thriving as a mother. For me, this disease gave me an excuse for not doing certain things. There would be days that I didn't feel like being responsible for my basic necessities, such as working out, cleaning the house, or making dinner. I let myself believe that it was because of my illness and that there was nothing I could do about it.

One day I decided not to let my thyroid condition control my life any longer. I needed to be intentional about each day and what I wanted to accomplish with it. Yes, being a mother is challenging, but it is the greatest blessing in the world. There is no greater privilege than to be given the opportunity to take care of and raise another little person. I couldn't waste that blessing, that privilege. I chose to be at my best every day.

What I would like to share with you are the ways in which I have been able to overcome my weaknesses. It took a lot of physical, mental, and emotional work, and it didn't happen overnight, but the life I'm living now is transformed. I'm happier and more productive and have greater peace of mind, in spite of my setback. I certainly don't have all of the answers but can provide some ideas for attaining and maintaining more energy and growth every day. As busy mothers, it is important to have a plan of action to overcome those difficult moments.

1.) Plan out your week so you wake up with an intention for everyday!
Waking up with an intention helps you have the clarity to initiate your day. Waking up with a specific focus for your day makes decisions easier, therefore giving you the opportunity to use your energy more effectively. What I like to do is plan out my week on Sunday by organizing each day so that I have less to worry about throughout the week. I wake up before my kids and structure my week as much as possible. I make it a point to place an intention for each day of the week. Then I can wake up with a purpose in mind. If you are ready to roll in the morning with a motivated intent, the likelihood of you wanting to stay in bed will diminish. An example of an intention would be "aspiring to make two new business contacts that day." You will be amazed at the feeling of excitement you get when you try this out! Give it a shot and see what happens*

If you don't plan for the week you are ultimately setting yourself up for failure. Strategic planning is one of the key components to living a life of freedom. When I say freedom I am referring to having freedom from the busyness. The world seems to get busier and busier all the time, therefore, requiring more energy. It is necessary to plan for success by adhering to a schedule that makes sense for your personal needs. When I work with many of my clients, they are working around other people's schedules instead of their own, which is much more challenging. My advice to them is to be sure to make a schedule based on their own needs and not someone else's. It will make you will feel much more comfortable, confident, and less stressed out.

2.) Concentrate on one thing at a time

I no longer believe in multitasking. I used to try to accomplish most tasks by completing them along with another task. Rarely did I feel good about the results because I was spreading myself thin and not giving a full focus to any one thing. You compromise your thoughts when you try to multitask. It just doesn't work. It never did and never will because our minds are not wired that way. I know it sounds crazy, but the more you give attention to one thing at a time, the more energy you will have because your mind will not be overwhelmed by everything else you are trying to achieve at that moment. Note: you must finish the first task to feel that sense of relief in order to move on to the next unless you are working on a larger long-term goal. Then you must break that task up into smaller easy-to-manage tasks. For example, writing a book. Instead of telling yourself you need to finish the whole thing to feel relief, break it down into chapter goals. When you complete your goal for one specific chapter, you can move forward on to the next task with ease. This can apply to home and work projects as well.

3.) Become selective with what you spend your time on during the day.

Let's talk about Instagram, for example, or any other of your preferred social media platforms. Every time you flip through the feed you are making a decision to read the content and look at the pictures. This is something we all do. It's part of the social media craze. I want to you to reflect upon that. Ask yourself how much time you are actually spending flipping through each post. It consumes a lot of energy and time that you could be spent doing something else, like spending quality time with your family.

If you are going to look at Instagram, I want you to be selective and not to allow yourself to get consumed. A kind of "get in get out" philosophy.

Also, consider what responsibilities can be outsourced when it comes to decision-making. Areas of your work (inside and outside of the home) that are a pain for you to do can cause energy drain, so it is very beneficial to consider other options. The way I see it, if it is not in some way educating, helping, or inspiring you or your family then you are wasting your time. We have so little of it anyway, why waste it on something that is going to make no impact on you now or ever? Don't waste time, embrace the hours of the day and do the things that make sense on a daily basis. I always consider my family first so that helps me make decisions on what to rid myself of. I would encourage you to do the same. I try to involve my family in a lot of what I do in my business. I make sure that some of the things I do can go hand in hand with my kid's day to day routine. For example, bringing my kids to the library to play when I am writing an excerpt from my book can kill two birds with one stone.

4.) Give yourself "ME" time every day.
I know sometimes it seems impossible to do this, especially with children, but it is essential to your personal well-being. Prayer and meditation have done wonders for me. Even taking the time to go outside and pick some flowers or walking through a garden can completely invigorate you. Spending time in nature for me is essential to my soul. I now wake up every day between 5:00 and 5:30 A.M. and spend time on myself. I thought when I started doing this that I would be exhausted later in the day, but to my surprise, I have just as much energy as if I slept until 6:30 A.M. The difference is that I can have my whole day planned out and ready to go before my three kids wake up. I can't even begin to tell you how much better my days have been after making the decision to wake up at this time because that is when I am able to take time for myself. Are some days harder than others? Absolutely! But I know that taking this time for myself is essential for my well-being and productivity throughout the day. Even a little bit of time goes a long way!

5.) Pray to God for Wisdom, Direction, and Protection.
I see life similar to how Mrs. Gump did in Forrest Gump. She said, "Life is like a box of chocolates. You never know what you're going to get." What a true statement that is. We don't know what kind of

cards we will be dealt. We go through many ups and downs and sometimes the storms last a long time. In some of the most difficult moments, nothing but prayer can give you the peace and comfort you are yearning for. There have been times I could not sleep because I could not stop worrying about my kids. There is always so much to think about. If they are sick or something is actually the matter you may as well forget sleeping! But God provides a blessing over our lives and understands everything we are going through. If we put our trust in Him and ask for His wisdom and guidance, He provides us the tools to know what to do in even the most difficult of circumstances.

One of the things I pray for the most is to get through the day. Sometimes when I wake up in the morning, the day can seem so daunting. I feel overwhelmed with tasks that seem to be constantly looming over me. It is during those times of frustration and chaos that we need to be still and remember we are human. We are only capable of doing so much in a single day. There are only 24 hours that allow us to accomplish tasks and achieve goals. Some of that time even needs to be dedicated to beauty rest! Wisdom, direction, and protection are among the most noteworthy requests we can present to God.

As a parent, we are constantly striving to provide our children with wisdom and guidance, by showing them the way and helping them make good decisions. We want to give them the tools they need to be successful and we desire to always protect them as they grow. We never know what kind of circumstances they will be presented within life, so praying about safety is always a good thing. In those moments, prayer surrounds me like a cloud of peace. If we desire these things for our children, how much more does our Heavenly Father wish to give these things to us and our children? Prayer is a way in which we can ask and receive peace, wisdom, guidance, safety, and sanity!

There is no question that parenting is challenging, whether you are a stay at home mom or a working parent. It is never easy in either circumstance. It always seems as though there is so much to do and so little time. My hope for you today is that you would feel the strength in knowing that you are enough and that your kids love you more than you can imagine. It may not seem like it, but all the effort that you put forth day in and day out to provide, pamper, love, and discipline your kids does not go unseen. Remember the uniqueness you provide as a mother and the gifts you have been given to use them when raising the children you were blessed with.

Confession #8 Open Adoption Is the Answer
Deborah Kenny

I am the proud single mother of a truly remarkable daughter. It's been her and I from the beginning. Unfortunately, her father has been absent most of her life. Life has not been easy but by God's grace, he has always supplied our needs. As a young girl, it's been really hard for her with no male presence. So not having that balance she searched for love and approval in the wrong places.

During her freshman year in high school, she became pregnant. We didn't even realize it until she was 5 months pregnant. She was in shock and I was devastated. I knew I could not afford to take care of this child and she was a child herself.

Our first course of action was to visit a pregnancy facility to find out how far along she was and what our options were. First, was the ultrasound where we confirmed she was five months along. Then we sat down with this counselor who proceeds to tell my 15 year old that the state would pay for everything and she could continue with her life the way it was, from high school, friends, then college, and so on. I don't know what world this woman lived in but who in their right mind would tell a teenager this bunch of unrealistic things and sugar coat everything. Then there was the option for abortion.

Needless to say, I pulled the women in the hallway and explained to her this was a total lie and I would take it from here and we left.

Well, I just sat down and cried to the Lord for direction on how to help my daughter and unborn grandchild in this situation.
Every summer my daughter and I would go to our church Christian camp. Myself as a counselor and her being a camper. Needless to say, this all happened 1 week before we were going. So off we went. During the week at camp, we always have a Holy Spirit night which falls on Wednesday.

1000 kids were there and during praise and worship time and I knew my daughter was falling apart but I couldn't find her. When I finally did she was on the floor with a Pastor praying over her. I held her tight while I whispered in her ear God's got us and he will bring us through. As the night continued we received a message and afterwards went to the activity center for some snacks. My daughter went off with her friends and I walked to the back of the building and just fell apart. I prayed the god would reveal to me his will for our circumstance.

What I did know is that I could not afford daycare, food or healthcare for this child. We had no family support. I just did not know what to do. As I leaned against that building crying and completely at a loss a pastor came walking up actually it was the same pastor who had been praying over my daughter hours earlier and asked what was going on. So I told him. He showed such compassion and was truly concerned. This pastor shared with me about open adoption?? I had no idea something like this existed. It's when a birth mother, grandmother and family members can actually continue a relationship with her daughter, my granddaughter, even though she has been adopted by another family.

This pastor actually got me in touch with a birth mother, adopted daughter and adoptive mother who explained to me how wonderful this experience had been for all 3 of them. This situation had created such security in the child, knowing that her mom loved her but could not take care of her so she selflessly did what was best for her.

Everyone won and was so happy. The next course of action was to go to my pastor and seek direction. My pastor suggested I go to Bethany Christian Adoption Agency. So I called them to see how this actually works. They explained that my daughter would have a choice of parents to pick from based on a biography that they wrote explaining who they were and what they could offer this child. At this point god put this in my heart that this was his will and I would have to take the next step and explain this to my daughter.

I was totally confused on how to do this. God guided me to one of my Christian sister that explained to me that I had to give her choice. Either an open adoption or a single women's facility to raise her daughter. She had to take responsibility for this situation.

Well, I sat down and gave her these choices. It was the hardest thing I ever had to do as a mom. She was so upset that I asked her to give up her child it was so difficult. However, after explaining to her these were her options because I could not afford this and it was not my responsibility but hers and the consequences in keeping this child would be dropping out of school getting job and no college or future she decided that an open adoption was the best option for her daughter.

Our next step was to make an appt. with Bethany Christian Adoption Agency, which we did. At our first meeting, my daughter was given 3 books of a profile on each family. We both read all 3 and upon finishing she decided to with the family that had 3 children so her daughter would have siblings to play with. From there, our counselor arranged our first meted and we met at Panera Bread. The adoptive parents were very compassionate know we did not want to do this but knew in our hearts this was the right thing to do. It would give my daughter a relationship with her daughter as well as a future, and she could carry on and create her own future. As my daughter talked and asked questions like who would name the baby my daughter and adoptive mother decided to name her together.

So the adoptive mother picked a name and they both loved it and together they decided to give her, her birth mother's name. I thought this was awesome. My granddaughter would have a piece her mother for the rest of her life.

We continued to talk about their lives and what they did as a family. What they did for a living and about their kids. They were both teachers. This was wonderful. They both coached different teams for extra money, the dad, softball club teams and, the mom, volleyball club teams.

They were just nice people whose hearts were Christ-centered and they wanted to help us. In that moment we knew, they were the ones. The next get together they would be bringing their kids. We decided to meet at the aquarium downtown. It was a lovely day. The kids were awesome, kind, and so polite. We took pictures and talked to them about what they liked to do. It was a lot of fun. My daughter fell in love with all of them and so did I.

On the next get together we would meet at their home. At that time we met the future grandparents, the adoptive parents siblings, and their kids. All of them were so compassionate toward my daughter and I. It was simply confirmation, this was the right family and my granddaughter would be very happy here.

By this time we were getting closer to the birth date. The adoptive parents and my daughter decided she would keep the baby for the first week and then turn her over. I actually suggested this because I thought it would be good for my daughter to experience the responsibility that goes into taking care of a newborn. After this, she really understand that she needed a safe, secure Christ-centered home if she was going to bring a child into this world.

She wanted to have a family like the adoptive family, Christ-centered mom, dad, and siblings. I am a single mother and I was not able to give her the father she so desperately needed. However, now my granddaughter will have a great future. My daughter could go to college and create the future God intended her to have.

The baby was born in December right around Christmas. She was beautiful just like her mother. As planned, we kept her for a week. After the first night, my daughter asked me how I did this alone. I informed her it was very hard but I was 37 years old, had a good job, and a secure home for her to grow up in. She never realized the responsibility. During this one week, we had her we had her blessed on Sunday which happened to be Christmas Day. My Pastor told our story and let's just say there was not a dry eye in the house. On the morning of December 26 that year we turned her over to the adoptive parents. My daughter and I were very sad but both knew we did the right thing.

We were able to see her the following week on New Year's Day. It was great! Life moved on and we saw her quite frequently. This is the most graceful relationship my daughter and I have ever experienced. My granddaughter calls me Nana and my daughter Mommy. She is such a joy and a blessing.

My daughter is now in her junior year of college studying business. She has a bright future ahead of her and so does my granddaughter.

GOD IS SO GOOD.

Confession #9 The Bigger Picture
Erica Coghlan

I was very excited when I found out I was pregnant with my second child. The beginning of the pregnancy went smoothly. I did experience morning sickness, but that was to be expected. The only concern I had was that I have a history of depression and I had been taking medication. I decided to get off it when I got pregnant because it wasn't safe for the baby. At first, I was okay. That changed as I got further along in my pregnancy.

When I was in my second trimester, I started feeling symptoms of depression arise. I dealt with it, attributing it to being hormonal and having over the top emotions. I continued to feel down and I cried a lot. It got to the point where I didn't want to be alone while my husband was at work. I would spend the night at my parents' house when he worked late. I knew I couldn't go on like this; it wasn't good for me or the baby. I decided to call my obstetrician.

My doctor told me that going off antidepressants is difficult. She felt that my health and mental state are important, as well as the health of my unborn baby. If the rest of the pregnancy was to go well, I needed to be well too! She put me on a different medication that would not be a risk to the baby. It helped me very much. I was able to move on and be happy again. Things were looking up. I thought all of my problems were behind me.

Everything was going well. The baby was developing right on track and the medication was keeping depression at bay. It looked like I was having a normal pregnancy and delivery. However, that was not in the cards for me. At 33 weeks pregnant, complications arose.

I came back from a birthday party and I felt off. In addition to aches and pains, I noticed a lot of swelling in my legs and feet. I also felt short of breath. I called my doctor's office and was told that those symptoms are common in pregnancy. I had a doctor's appointment the following week. I was told not to worry but to call back if the symptoms got worse. They didn't but the symptoms continued and overall I just didn't feel well. I kept getting more and more concerned and couldn't stop worrying until the day of my appointment. Sure enough, when I arrive at my appointment, my blood pressure was sky-high. I was sent over to the hospital to be monitored. My primary doctor was not on call, but I was seen by another physician. I spent 4 hours there and then they discharged me. I was told to go back to the doctor's office in two days to have my pressure checked. I thought that since they discharged me everything was fine. I thought the doctor was just being cautious by asking me to return and I expected my blood pressure to go down. I was wrong! The next morning I received a call from the nurse at my doctor's office. She did not agree with the doctor that had examined me and said I should not have been sent home. She told me to go back to the hospital.

I didn't want to go back. I wanted to stay home. I was feeling much better and I didn't want to sit around and wait at the hospital for hours only to be sent home again. I didn't think the situation was that serious. Being at the hospital made me very uncomfortable and anxious so I was worried going back would cause my blood pressure to rise. Since I already had an appointment the following day, I waited until then to see the doctor.

Boy, was I wrong again! It was at that appointment that I was diagnosed with preeclampsia. This time, I couldn't get out of going to the hospital. I was to be admitted for a few days and I was on bed rest until further notice.

I went in thinking I would be monitored for a few hours and my pressure would go down. I was only 34 weeks pregnant at this point. The baby couldn't come yet! My blood pressure stayed high and I didn't know what to expect. Of course, worrying about it probably wasn't helping my blood pressure go down at all! Next thing I know the nurse comes in and tells me I'm going to labor and delivery. I was surprised and a little scared.

When I got up to labor and delivery I was told that I would continue to be monitored. If my pressure didn't go down, I would have to be induced. Suddenly, this all got real. My baby could be coming 6 weeks early! I was glad to be on antidepressants at the time because my emotions were a wreck.

Those hours were some of the longest in my life. There was no change. In the wee hours of the morning, it was decided. I would be induced. I was a ball of fear and nerves, but luckily the labor and delivery went well. My baby boy was born and I was the proud, anxious mother of a preemie. I only got to hold him for a little while before he was whisked off to the NICU.

The hardest part of having a premature baby is leaving the hospital without them! I spent all day, every day at the NICU while he was there. I hated having to leave him every night as visiting hours ended. I knew he was well cared for by the nurses on staff, but it was still hard leaving him. I was so lonely. My husband was at work and my daughter was staying with my parents. I was feeling depressed once more. I had already struggled with postpartum depression after I had my daughter. This time I was already on medication so thankfully it didn't come on very strong. But I needed to be with my baby. Just holding him lifted my spirits. On top of that, I missed my daughter and felt bad for not being with her. When I was at home, I missed my little boy.

After 16 days, my son was able to come home. We were a family again! I cried so many tears of joy that day. What I went through was difficult. Those two and a half weeks felt like years! It could have been worse; some moms have to wait months to bring their preemies home. I learned that every pregnancy is different. Depression hurts but with proper supervision and cooperation with your doctor, you can get through it.

Not needing antidepressants and having the perfect labor story used to be some of my biggest concerns and highest priorities. But after everything I've gone through, my perspective has changed. Depression and a complicated pregnancy are small issues in the grand scheme of things. Having a preemie isn't easy, but now I look at my two kids and I know I am truly blessed, despite the hardships I've had to endure. You never know what life has in store for you.

The bigger picture is being a good mom. I try to do that every day! I hope that my story inspires and encourages you when hard times and complications come your way. Even when the nights are long and you feel more alone than ever before, know that the struggles are worth it in the end.

Confession #10 I'm Not An Alcoholic
April O'Leary

I was 29 years old and pregnant with my third daughter, filling out the forms at the first prenatal visit. I wrote a big zero next to "Number of drinks you consume daily."

"Who drinks daily?" I thought.

I remember my college days of binging on weekends and blacking out, sometimes not knowing how I got home, but that was light years ago.

I had had a spiritual awakening when my father was diagnosed with cancer just three years prior. Drinking dropped out of my life. I had also dropped out of college, gotten engaged and was going to be a missionary to save the world.

But God had other plans for me.

After a broken engagement, I re-enrolled in night school to finish my degree in Education, was working full-time during the day and making time to see my dad as he went through cancer treatments at the University of Chicago Hospital.

No time for drinking. No time for friends. No time for fun. Life was all work and no play.

My dad and I often had heated theological discussions. I would throw out scriptures like, "God wishes above all things that you prosper and be in good health even as your soul prospers.". He would talk about Paul's thorn which God never removed. He believed that if God wanted him healed he would do it, and if he didn't he saw this life as temporary and knew that all are healed when they pass on to eternal life.

Unfortunately, my father passed away at the age of 48. I felt lost. I couldn't understand why a loving God wouldn't heal his child. I tried to hang onto the faith that fired inside of me. The faith that was calling me to the mission field. The faith that showed up through the gifts of the spirit and miraculous healing. Didn't Jesus even say, John 14:12 "These things I have done, even greater things shall you do?"

Yeah. Well, the fire in me slowly died with my dad's death and my missionary dreams went with it.

I met Jim while on vacation eight weeks later. I was 21, and he was 29. He was tall and handsome and drove a nice car. He asked me to dinner and we had a good time.

After a rocky courtship we got married when I was six months pregnant with our first daughter Sadie. Seventeen months later Molly followed. I poured myself into motherhood. From playgroups to library story times, to dance classes and even being president of our local Moms' Club, I was burning the candle at both ends.

I was trying to be perfect. Maybe you've done that too? I never asked for help, never hired a babysitter or cleaning service and we never made it a priority to schedule a date night.

Resentment started to set in. Once again my life was all work and no fun. I was burning out fast.

My one escape was a monthly MOMS Club book group. We rotated houses and signed up to bring food and drinks. Drinks, yes, that was the answer to the pent up frustration, exhaustion, and guilt I was feeling. A few drinks with the moms and I felt like my old self. Funny. Carefree. Young. Reckless.

And I was reckless.

Once I turned ON the switch to "party mode" (even just at book club) there was no OFF switch. The same patterns I experienced in college surfaced again. Blackouts and driving home.

I remember hating the question, "Did you read the book?"

Sometimes I did, but most of the time, I admitted I didn't. It became a joke. I was there for the drinking. Wasn't everyone?

The monthly binging continued, without a hitch. I looked forward to it. It was a light on often dark days. Drinkers find other drinkers to drink with too.

Luckily we had some neighbors who would come over to our house once the kids were in bed and we'd stay up drinking until the wee hours of the morning. It's a modern-day miracle that the kids didn't wake up and God knows I wouldn't have been able to take care of them.

You can suspect there's a problem with alcohol if the point of your social life (in your mind) is to drink. But I didn't realize that at the time.

At this point, I was stressed out, felt totally unappreciated and almost invisible. My two big girls were in elementary school so I took a very part-time job teaching preschool with the hopes of building up my resume so I could resume teaching when my youngest, Amy, went into Kindergarten.

One of the perks was Amy got to attend for free and the downside was I was only paid $65/week. I tried quitting several times and they begged me to stay. So I did.

My marriage was on the rocks too. After an annual doctor's visit, Jim made a mature decision to get on a healthier path. He decided to quit drinking before it became a problem. Yay Jim. Or not. When you're a drinker, having a dry husband is not what you're looking for in a partner!

What was I going to do? A solution appeared out of nowhere. I still remember the life changing conversation I had with a friend just like it was yesterday. She saw my stress said, "Just have a drink in the afternoon."

Is that allowed, I thought.

I was raised a rule-follower and it never occurred to me to drink alone while I was home with the girls. What an epiphany! Sounded like a plan to me. A ~~damn~~ good plan!

Then the carpooling started. At 4pm my carpooling friend and I would hang out and drink. Either I was dropping off at her house or she was dropping off at mine. Our kids loved playing together and we loved Captain Morgan and Diet Coke. It was a win-win relationship.

It's funny how sneaky alcohol can creep into an otherwise normal life. It speaks to you. It tells you everything will be okay. Just relax. You deserve it. You work so hard. Take a break.

It presents itself as a solution to your problems.

Never mind that it's actually preventing you from dealing with your problems.

Never mind that it's making you more irritable.

Never mind that your personality changes when you drink.

Never mind that you're more permissive with your kids.

Never mind that you sometimes drive after you've had more than a few.

Never mind that you used to buy the skinny bottle of Captain Morgan, and now you buy the handle bottle because it's only $3 more. You'll never finish all that, anyway.

Never mind you finish it before the week is over and feel guilty. Surely, you don't need that again.

Then, you're back. Of course you're buying *that one* again. After all, you have friends coming over for happy hour today.

It's a slippery slope, and before you know it, you think back to that prenatal visit where they asked, "How many drinks a day do you have?" and you wonder if you have a problem. But you probably don't. After all, everyone else drinks as much or more than you anyways.

Our marriage literally hit rock bottom when Jim stopped drinking. I was confused and annoyed and frankly just plain bored. I had an affair and we almost ended up divorced. Thankfully it led me to a therapy office where I learned about codependency and how to let go of unhealthy guilt.

That new-found knowledge changed my outlook on life. Our marriage got back on track. I decided to pursue a degree in Life Coaching and a year later opened a practice to help other moms who were struggling with self-care, parenting and relationship problems. I was once again going to save the world. I built a website and was seeing private clients. I wrote a few self-help books and spoke on national radio shows. I even ran my own mom conferences.

I was 100% happy on the outside. From professional headshots to business clothes, and speaking gigs you would have thought I had arrived. But my drinking continued. It was always rearing its ugly head at the most inopportune moments.

In the church I grew up in drinking was not allowed at all. And definitely not at church functions! Ironically enough my daughters went to a private Methodist school. One where drinking was permitted. I had no idea that concept even existed. But at this school alcohol was a critical component of many big fundraisers which brought in hundreds of thousands of dollars. I was definitely in the right place.

I can remember one particular event where I was dressed in denim and diamonds, and was so eager to get to the open bar and get the evening started.

When I looked over, the pastor of the church was standing right there next to me. I felt so awkward!

He said, "Go ahead get whatever you want. It's on me!" We both laughed. That was all the permission I needed to spend the entire evening right out there by the bar. I missed the entire dinner and by the end of the night was stumbling out without my shoes on.

Jim said the next day, "I'm so embarrassed you're my wife!"

I didn't do anything illegal, I thought.

I called a few friends to find out what happened and asked if I did anything embarrassing. Not that they could remember. And one friend reassured me I wasn't the worst one there and joked that I was really funny. Good to know!

So I guess Jim was wrong. It was his problem if he doesn't want to have a good time.

Yeah, that was me. One too many binge episodes. One too many drives without getting caught. One too many poor decisions.

I tend to minimize most things in life, but that last drive is etched in my brain. Another harmless night at a family dinner with no intention of drinking too much, but I turned the switch on, and alas, it wouldn't turn off.

Driving my minivan down the highway, cruise set at the speed limit, I cracked the window, turned off the radio and had both hands on the wheel. Then I looked over at my 13 year old daughter in the seat next to me and saw a face I'll never forget it. It's like, somehow, she knew.

I thought to myself, *this night could truly screw up the rest of my life. What if someone hit me? What if I drove off the road? What if I got pulled over? I could kill them or myself or someone else. I could end up in jail; ruin my career I'd been working so hard to build the past 7 years. Holy crap, what am I doing? She deserves better than this!*

I could just keep ignoring it and hope I'd keep dodging the bullets or I could decide to take a good hard look at the facts. Decades of drunk driving. Never a DUI or a night in jail. Yet so many moments I didn't remember. Times I could have ruined my life. But for the grace of God it hadn't happened...YET.

The game is up, Dr. Jekyll and Mr. Hyde.

That night, I got home safely. Parked my van in the driveway, from what I remember, and swore I would never drink again. I didn't know if I had a problem but I was willing to be honest and try to deal with the facts.

So I showed up at our local 12-step club the next morning and cried. I hardly remember what was said. I was given a pamphlet for women, and in it were 15 questions from an Ann Landers column, to help you see if you were truly an alcoholic.

There it was in black and white. I couldn't deny it. I started piecing together the scenes of the past, and although I was, quote, "dry" for a good number of years in my 20s, I can see that the compulsion had always been there, even as far back as 15 year olds drinking at a friend's house to blackout and vomiting.

Throughout my life, I would swing from one extreme to the other. I just can do medium very well. I later found out that is also an alcoholic trait.

I'm so grateful that today, my girls never have to see me drink again. I'm so grateful that today I can set an example for them of what healthy, responsible living is all about. I'm so grateful I have learned how to solve my problems with a program and steps that work.

Today I don't wish I could escape the hard moments of life with alcohol. I don't naively think they will go away without me doing anything to change myself or my circumstances. My life is 100% congruent. Who I am on the outside is who I am on the inside. No more hiding.

I'm not ashamed to admit I have the disease of alcoholism.

I didn't choose it. I see now that it has always been a part of my makeup even from my early days. My body doesn't metabolize alcohol the way a normal person's body does. It creates an allergic reaction which tells it to consume more, not to stop. I had no idea that was happening all along.

Today I'm grateful, through the grace of God, I was able to identify a moment of clarity and that with His help, I got off the elevator before a car wreck or a detox center or jail or death. So many are not so fortunate.

This disease has helped me to rediscover who God is and seek His help every day in a way I never have before. I feel the freedom to love others without judgment and allow them to walk their own path knowing that God has a plan for them too.

I pray for those who are out there, still sick and suffering. May they also have their own moment of clarity and act on it. May we as compassionate human beings see them as sick not bad.

Finally, I pray for every mom reading this, that she may find peace and happiness in the presence of God as she understands him, and not in the false hope and promises of alcohol.

Your kids deserve all of you.

April O'Leary is a best-selling author and life and business coach. Her latest book The Ultimate Love Affair: Awaken to God's Love Within in 40 Days is available at www.ultimateaffairbook.com.

Confession #11 "Rainbow Child"
Francielle Daly

After being pregnant once, you kind of understand how it will go the second time around. Although, every "first" is still exciting from the first kicks to hearing the heartbeat for the first time. Oh that heartbeat!!! Seeing the feet and hands grow after each ultrasound, I mean, being pregnant is pretty amazing. But, for my second time around, the morning sickness was brutal, and I was consistently in the bathroom or in bed. All I did was go to work and come home to sleep and try to keep food down. I just wanted to feel good. Finally after fourteen weeks, I started to feel better.

My fiancé, now husband, was an amazing supporter. He was super excited since this was his first child and he accompanied me at every doctor appointment. When I needed something, he got it for me. My midwife was amazing too; she was on top of it all and every time I saw her she was warm and welcoming. I selected this office because they had midwives and I was going to deliver my baby at an awesome hospital. Everything I imagined and wanted to happen was happening. As I was experiencing this second pregnancy, I was also being mom to my first daughter. We were getting ready for Kindergarten! She was my "big girl" and she was going to be a big sister. She was as excited as me and my fiancé were about all the new changes.

Then, August 21, 2013 happened. I remember it very clearly. It was my daughter's first day of Kindergarten and I was able to take her to her first day of school. I took pictures outside when she went to line up, went to the classroom with her and met her teacher. I had my cute little baby bump and was 20 weeks pregnant. I felt the baby move a few weeks prior to this and at my 18 week check-up, listened to the heartbeat. With this being my fiancé's first child, I wanted it to be special. Since this was my second, I wanted to do things a little different. I only had a small baby shower for my first born and was very young at the time. My future mother- in-law and I planned a gender reveal party for later that day, because I had a 12 o'clock ultrasound appointment scheduled to find out what the gender was. I planned to ask the technician to write the gender down and then give it to my future mother-in-law to reveal to all the family and friends that would be there later for the party.

There we were sitting in the ultrasound room. I was lying down on the bed with my shirt pulled above my baby bump and my fiancé standing at my side. We were both anxiously waiting. The ultrasound technician rubbed jelly on my belly and put the sonogram on it. There we saw our baby looking hunched over and sleeping. I will never forget the words I said, "Oh little one, wake up! We need to find out what you will be!" I was telling the ultrasound tech we had a gender reveal party waiting for us. As she circled the sonogram around on my belly and wiggled it, her face became white as snow. I knew something was wrong and then came the words you never want to hear, "I am so sorry, but your baby has no heartbeat!" My throat became parched. My heart sank. I started to shake. I said, "EXCUSE me, you said what?"

I didn't get it. What did I do wrong? Why was there no heartbeat? What was going on? The ultrasound tech said she would get the Doctor on duty to come talk to us and give us the final word. I looked over at my fiancé and he looked completely puzzled. He asked me what it meant that the heartbeat stopped. I guess he didn't comprehend what she told us. I swallowed really hard while holding back all the tears. I felt like I needed to be somewhat strong and said, "our baby has no heartbeat and that means our baby is gone, it's dead." He fell into my arms and cried. He didn't understand what happened either. The door opened and the doctor and ultrasound technician walked in. The words every pregnant woman dreads hearing were then spoken, "Yes, it's confirmed your baby is dead. The cause of this is unknown, but we can start testing and possibly figure out what happened.

We said yes for all tests to be done to figure out what had happened to our baby. We were also given two choices; to deliver the baby or have a DNC. If we chose a DNC, they would put me to sleep and get rid of the baby. I opted for a DNC, because I could not bear the pain to deliver a dead baby and this thought still breaks me. Since I chose a DNC, I had to go home with my baby in my belly for two more days due to the availability of their schedule. While writing this, I still can't believe I had to go home with our dead baby inside me.

There I was leaving the ultrasound room with news that are unborn baby was actually dead and still did not know what the gender was. I couldn't feel anything at that moment. I was so numb. I went to the bathroom before leaving the ultrasound and texted a couple friends right away. The texts back where all of shock and confusion. How in the world had I made it so far without seeing there was some type of complication. I just felt the baby move a couple weeks prior and it was the best feeling! Now, I felt nothing. The car ride back was a quiet one. I will never forget the words that came out of my fiancé's mouth, "Why won't God let me have a child of my own?" I was filled with so many emotions, I was so unsure, and I was so in shock.

We stopped at my parents' house first and I had already text my mom. The moment I walked in, I saw my daughter's face. She was unsure what was going on. She was old enough to understand mommy was having a baby but to start explaining there was no heartbeat and how it happened. I was not sure where to even start. My dad took me in his arms as well as my mom, and I just sobbed.

This was by far the worst day of my life. When we explained to my daughter her sister or brother decided it wasn't time to come and he or she went back to heaven, she understood but was disappointed and sad. She cried too, but I don't think she truly understood entirely everything that was happening. She could see and sense that mommy needed her more at this moment and held me.

We went back to my fiancé's house and knew what to expect. We prepared ourselves as best as possible, but honestly how could we really prepare with the news being so recent. We walked into the house decorated with blue and pink ALL around us. I was so mad and had to fight back the tears as my future mother-in-law asked us for the envelope and how the ultrasound went. I choked on my words and my fiancé told her the news. She cried with us. It was a moment where we just felt comfort and love. We chose not to send anymore texts or to make any calls because everyone was already on their way to the house.

The doorbell rang and the smiles, joy, and congratulations came in. As people walked into the house, my tears just kept coming. I wanted to run and shut myself in my room, but I knew the best thing for me was to be around others and simply accept their love and comfort. After the warm welcome, we went ahead and told everyone the unexpected news. There was no amount of words anyone could say to make this day any easier. I honestly didn't want to hear anything and I just needed the support that day. They ate, I snacked, and then within hours our family and friends were gone.

I was still not sure what I felt, but I remember my fiancé typing away on his phone to let EVERYONE else know what was going on. Just weeks before we shared the exciting news that we were expecting and shared about our gender reveal party.

Then my fiancé posted on social media, "Today Francielle & I were presented with the news that our unborn child does not have a heartbeat. Meaning it's possible we lost our expecting child. Even with faith the size of a mustard seed we are unsure how to discern being with the news and how to, or when to, let go and believe in miracles like Lazarus, being risen from the dead. Please pray and align with us as we believe like Lazarus, for our miracle. All glory to you Lord of All. In Jesus name."

The comments and messages flooded in and we received a phone call from a friend of ours from our old church. She prayed for us as many were praying for us, and believed our baby would come alive like Lazarus.

The Bible says if you have faith even as small as a mustard seed you can move mountains. At that very moment that is what I felt and believed. I had faith, I knew God, and I loved God but what I also had was a little doubt. The Bible also says, "You don't have enough faith," Jesus told them. "I tell you the truth, if you had faith even as small as a mustard seed, you could say to this mountain, 'Move from here to there,' and it would move. Nothing would be impossible." Matthew 17:20 (NLT) There I was on the floor, praying, crying, and believing for a miracle. I knew I was blessed with my daughter but still so many emotions ran through my head and in my heart.

Finally, Friday came and I had an appointment with the high-risk OB/GYN. As I walked in the first thing I asked was if they could do an ultrasound to make sure the baby did not have a heartbeat. The ultrasound again confirmed our baby was not moving and had no heartbeat. I knew in that moment I was going to be taken down to surgery so they could take our baby out of me. As I was being put to sleep, I looked over and knew that the man next to me was the man I was going to spend the rest of my life with. This was not the first or last of struggles for us. If we could get through this then we can get through anything.

As I woke up from surgery, I saw a vision of me playing on a swing set and I was SUPER happy. I knew at that moment I was going to be okay and God was with me. About a month later, I received a phone call from the hospital and they informed me there were no abnormal findings with our baby boy. The gender was a boy and I was very heartbroken since I always wanted a boy. I had to go through each emotion as they came. I knew if I kept anything in I would go crazy! As time and months passed I kept the faith, but I will confess there were moments I was angry and couldn't understand why.

As time passed, I enjoyed every moment of life. This experience allowed me to see life differently and brought me closer to God. I was already a believer in Christ, but in these tough moments if you truly don't have a savior you can run to and simply share and scream and just speak with, then you could turn to so many other sources which could eventually destroy your life. Thankfully, I stayed focused and kept my eyes on the one above. Sure in some moments I did drift away but once you are truly walking with God it's so hard to stray away. The moments you have with God are unexplainable and something you crave for.

Our son was due on January 19, 2014. We thought he would be born on January 11, 2014 because my fiancé and I had a thing with the number eleven. In December 2013, I took a personal development class called the "Love Course" and breakthrough after breakthrough happened and in that class, I received the most powerful thing ever. I was able to share with a room full strangers that my son's heartbeat stopped because my son's heartbeat stopped. NOTHING MORE added. This was a huge breakthrough because for months I assumed it was something I ate or did that may have caused his heartbeat to stop. I had been trying to blame myself, but at that moment I was given permission to simply say his heartbeat stopped because it stopped. WOW!

It was like something was lifted up. I was able to look up and forward to so much more hope. Yes, I had God but God knew I needed some more tools which is why he brought me to this class. I was surrounded by others that supported me on this journey. The class was only a weekend long, but it life changing. Shortly after taking this class, I told my fiancé, "I'm ready to get married." We were already engaged, but I was the one on hold with planning our wedding because I was stuck. This course helped me to finally be freed up of my emotions and to move on. I was now ready to write the next chapter in my life. The chapter God had been wanting to continue. I was stuck in emotion and regret, which was not God's plan for me and he wanted to take those feelings away from my life. I knew all of this but when you're in the midst of things, you forget you need something to remind you and shake you up a bit.

My fiancé and I got married on January 11, 2014. The day we thought our baby boy in Heaven would be born was actually a day we were able to celebrate both his life and the beginning to ours as The Daly's. Looking back on all this, I am super thankful for this trial in my life. It didn't break me, and it led me to a life which was stronger in Christ. It made me a person who had a mission.

A few months after our wedding, I received the best news and it was on Mother's day. I was pregnant! At first, the pregnancy was a little nerve wracking, but once I hit 21 weeks my husband and I were able to enjoy the thought of our new baby girl. We named her Genesis, our rainbow child.

So here's my question to you. What situation has happened to? Did you lose your faith? Did you lose the desire for something? Maybe you also had a miscarriage or lost a baby? It really doesn't matter how many weeks you were you still lost a baby you were hoping to meet one day and it did not happen! How have you allowed yourself to heal? Who or what are you leaning onto for that hope and healing?

Confession #12 "Life Whizzes By"
Beth Aldrich

Everything was a blur as I glimpsed at the lights on the ceiling of the emergency room. The ER doctors and nurses quickly and cautiously cut my fluffy gray cashmere sweater (now soaked in blood) right down the middle so they could carefully remove it. In shock, I babbled about my kids, a to-do list and asking, "Why am I here? What happened?" Once they assessed that I didn't have a broken neck, they confirmed that I had fractured a bone in my face and suffered several deep cuts on my face, including a completely severed lip. At that moment, I realized just how difficult it was to talk without a top lip! The feeling of fear took hold as I visualized.

They wheeled me on the flat gurney out of the ER and into a busy hallway, where I waited for the plastic surgeon on duty to put my face back together. For quite some time I waited in silence, perfectly still, as warm tears rolled down my face and into my ear. I glanced over at my husband who was holding vigil, protecting me and holding my hand. He didn't have to say a word because it was written all over his face. Silently my heartfelt his love. He told me, "Don't worry your face will heal in time; our children are so lucky they didn't lose you in the car accident today -- as am I. Everything will be okay." Then, I felt his grip on my hand tighten as he quickly removed a tear from the corner of his eye. His bravery and steadfast love is what got me through that terrible day.

Later that night, after the plastic surgeon had stitched up my face and reattached my lip, I was brought to my hospital room where my husband kissed me goodbye and promised to return the next day in hopes of taking me home. Now alone I was faced with my thoughts, an occasional attending nurse and the rhythmic pulse of the circulation machine pads, which were wrapped around my legs to ensure that I didn't get a blood clot. How did I get myself into this mess?

I remember getting into a cab to meet a film crew to work on a film segment for the Cool Globes summer lakefront exhibit (in Chicago) where we planned on meeting with then Mayor Daley—and the next thing I knew, my car smashed into another car. Wham! I hit the pixy-glass divider in the back seat. I remember hopping into a cab near my home on that snowy January day in Chicago as I checked my busy schedule on my hand-held device. I thought to myself, "There's just not enough time in the day... I have so much to do... pick up my sons at the bus, make dinner, exercise, do the laundry, write an article for my online magazine, work on the production sheet for my PBS TV series, sit, breathe, relax... how can I do it all?" Oh, such is the life of a Super Mom; trying to do it all, be it all and still fit into the perfect size dress. All these busy thoughts streamed through my head like an old-fashioned movie, while, in slow motion, I was flung forward, looking right into the eyes of the man driving the other car.

Three days later I came home from the hospital but was still a little wobbly. Each step shot pain through my body. Every motion pushed pain to every cut and bruise. I was "feeling sorry for myself as I entered the house and was greeted by my tail-wagging cocker spaniel, Barkley, who didn't seem to notice my face but appeared a little curious. My four-year-old son, on the other hand, innocently told me, "I love you mommy but I can't look at you because your face is scary." My heart sank, as he avoided my glances and turned away when I hugged him (for dear life). My two older sons were a bit braver. They were very curious about the details of the crash and my wounds. They assured me that my cuts looked "okay" and those they would heal, and then they were business as usual—reminiscent of what I had heard my husband say earlier that day. He coached them well.

As the days passed my stitches were removed and I began the process of getting my life back to normal. It was difficult to look in the mirror and see the new landscape of my face, so I decided to wait a few weeks before I really examined the damage. Instead, I concentrated on my family and home life. I spent extra time putting my sons to bed at night and my dog enjoyed the extra brushing and petting. What I discovered in my tender family moments was that, amidst the busy schedules and running around, we were all very happy. There was a feeling of joy and teamwork as we spent time together working on projects and playing. I slipped back into the regular mom I used to be when my sons were toddlers before I donned my cape and mask as Super Mom. It felt good. Good to be back in the center of it all—getting messy.

When did these layers of my life start to pile up? When did pregnancy turn into boo-boo kisser, story reader, ride-a-bike teacher, room mother, cookie maker, and homework queen and work-from-home media company owner? Then I realized—it's what I've dreamed about all of my life. When I was a little girl, I would do the apron, carry my baby doll, make pretend cookies, sweep the floor and play teacher, all in the same day. A-Ha! I've been a Super Mom since I was four! I've been rehearsing for this role for most of my life. I've juggled, multi-tasked and nurtured "babies" for as long as I can remember. People would ask me when I was younger what I wanted to be when I grew up. I would confidently tell them, "I want to be a mommy and help people."

That realization brought me to a special place. I decided to work from home and coach other moms, on healthy eating, living, and happiness. After studying holistic nutrition for a year, I became a

Certified Holistic Health Coach. While working with busy mom (while my kids were in school), I realized that I could best serve more women across the country by writing a "fun" healthy eating book. After hard work, determination, and many late-night writing sessions, I published my book, Real Moms Love to Eat: How to Conduct a Love Affair with Food, Lose Weight, and Feel Fabulous (Penguin/NAL, 2012). This book gave me the platform to create my own Food Strategy© Where I spoke to groups of women, appeared in media appearances across the country, sharing advice about living a balanced life in many aspects—not just through food.

I've always known that being a mother has given me a membership to the greatest club in the world. But what that accident on the snowy January day gave me was a sharp reminder that by simply loving and being with your kids, you ARE a Super Mom. Regardless of how many plates you keep spinning in the air, your children will love you for just being you, for being there, not somewhere else. I've discovered that by finding a way to work from home, I have been there when my sons needed me most. I set the schedule and make sure my days fits into theirs. Kids will always be proud of your accomplishments, but what REALLY matters to them is that you are at their side, as much as you can be and that you love them for being them, your Super Kids.

Life whizzes by, don't miss a minute of it.

Confession #13 "My Sons World"
Lia Jones

I am a pediatric speech therapist with 29 years of experience. I also had the pleasure of raising two sons. The story below is about my second son.

Beginning
In the spring of 1998, I was anxiously awaiting the birth of my second son. My first son was 27 months old. I was a stay at home mom at that time. I had thoroughly enjoyed watching my first son go through his developmental and communication milestones. He went through each one early or on time. He walked at a year; he had his first words around the same time. By the time he was 18 to 19 months old, he was able to say 7 to 10 word sentences (those sentences did not have perfect articulation but I was very proud). Part of the reason why my first son was such a percussionist early talker is because I am a pediatric speech therapist. By the time my second son was born, I had already been a speech therapist for nine years. I had worked diligently with my first son. The one on one attention helped his language to blossom. I was worried what the divided attention would do for my second son's development but expected something similar.

My first son was a very easy baby. He was easily soothed. He only asked to nurse once every three hours. He could sit quietly if he was not hungry in his baby swing for an hour with his favorite toy. He only cried when he absolutely needed my attention. As he grew we were able to spend afternoons looking at picture books and reading stories and working on language skills. He was able to attend weekly story-time at the library and the mornings at the local Mommy and Me group. I was overjoyed to find out I was expecting another son. I knew when I gave birth to my second son in the spring of 98 I would be experiencing identical joys of motherhood as with my first.

I could not wait to meet my second son. I was certain that raising him would be identical to the 27 months of joy I had experienced raising my first son.

In the spring of 1998, I gave birth via C-section. When I met him for the first time I was overjoyed by the small face resembling mine. He even had my dimple on his left cheek. I could not wait to bring this new addition to our family home.

Almost immediately I noticed this new baby was very different from the baby I had brought home just 27 months earlier. This baby cried. This baby cried a lot! I did not know how to comfort him. I tried all the things I had tried 27 months ago with my first son. I tried nursing him, changing him and putting him into the baby swing. He cried. I tried pacifiers and he cried. I tried swaddling him and he cried. I tried rocking him and he cried. I tried putting him up on my shoulder and he cried. I tried changing his diaper again and he cried. He just cried. He cried a lot. As a young mother, I was really perplexed. I knew I had done this before. I had done it very successfully before. I just couldn't understand what I was doing differently from what I had done just 27 months ago.

When my second son was around three months old, I took a part-time job as a speech therapist two evenings a week. I was only going to be gone from my family for about three hours. I left bottles and pacifiers for my husband to feed the baby. I trusted everything would be fine as I got ready to leave for work. I was looking forward to the 45 minute drive alone in my car. I was also excited to get back to the profession I absolutely loved. I had a great first night at work that is until I came home.

As I walked into my home I heard my son screaming. My husband said he's been crying since you left. I was horrified! My husband said, "I tried everything. I tried the bottles, I tried the pacifier, I tried a different pacifier, and I tried rocking and swaddling. Nothing calmed him down!" I raced upstairs to my crying baby. I picked him up and consoled him. I began to nurse him. He immediately stopped crying. The only way to calm my second son was to nurse him and to nurse him constantly. I nursed him consistently around the clock (every hour and a half). He would nurse 10 to 12 times a day. I began to realize he was not hungry, but he did not know how to maintain a calm state without nursing.

I was unable to work my part-time job. I couldn't leave my baby with a babysitter or with his father because they couldn't nurse him. So, I stayed home and I took care of my children.

As my son grew, I noticed that he was not developing language and words as easily as my first son. He did have advanced motor skills. He walked at nine months and was able to catch a ball at a year. Now, to be honest, there were definitely some differences in my parenting style between my first son and my second. My first was involved in different playgroups. I didn't have all the time I had to read picture books to my second son that I had for my first son.

When my second son was about nine months old he began to speak. He was able to say duck, truck and stuck. He also started to call me when he needed help. However, instead of calling me "mommy" or "mom". He called me "Ama". As a young mother, I thought this was very strange. As a speech therapist, I knew this was bizarre. I was extremely concerned about my son. However, I reminded myself he was only nine months old. I was certain he would develop more words as time went on. However, at 18 months old I noticed he had not learned any new words, and he was still calling me "Ama". I decided to borrow a screening test from work. I knew that it was not really the best thing for me to test my own child, but I had to know what was going on. After I gave my child the screening test I clearly saw he had a delay. The next day I went to work and asked my supervisor if she would send the evaluation team to my house. The date was arranged and my son was officially evaluated.

The evaluation team determined he had a language delay. I was right. They recommended that he receive speech therapy immediately. I was overjoyed. My son had been frustrated. He would sometimes cry because he did not have a language to express his thoughts and ideas. He babbled most of the time and had very few real words. I can remember when someone asked me why are you looking for a speech therapist for your child. Aren't you a speech therapist? Yes, I am I replied. However, it's important that I remain in the role of mother. While I was there as a child's speech therapist I was certainly not going to provide kisses to boo-boos, nutritious meals, and bedtime stories, those things needed to come from the parents. I knew my child needed me to be his mother.

My supervisor recommended a very good speech therapist who worked at a local preschool. I was excited. I called the preschool immediately and asked to speak to the speech therapist. She told me she was sorry, but she had no vacancies on her caseload. I would have to look elsewhere or go on a waiting list for speech therapy. I thought to myself there's no way my son can go on a waiting list. He's already frustrated. He already has a delay. He needs to have speech therapy right now! I thought to myself something has to be done. I thought to myself I can fix this. I said to her, "I'm a speech therapist I have 11 years of experience. I can work with children on your caseload. That would free up time in your schedule for you to work with my son. There was silence on the other end of the phone and then she said, "Let me talk to my supervisor. That may just work out." The next day she called to say that my idea would work out perfectly. Thank God! I thought to myself. There have been many times since that day that I have wondered what would have happened if I wasn't a speech therapist. What if I was an accountant? What if I was a nurse? What if I was in any other field other than a Speech Language Pathologist? What would have happened to my son?

My son began receiving speech therapy and in six months he began to turn the corner. He began calling me "mommy" and his vocabulary grew exponentially. He began putting two and three word sentences together. I was completely overjoyed. He began making requests. He began labeling items in the books. He began having conversations with me and his father and his brother. He began making friends in his playgroup. I was finally able to breathe a sigh of relief. We had turned the corner. Or so I thought so.

When my son was three years he began spinning uncontrollably. He would spin on anything that would turn. He would spin on his feet and on office chairs but his most favorite thing to spin on was a porch swing. He could spin on the porch swing for 15 or 20 minutes. I asked him, "How can you spin for that long? Are you feeling dizzy?" He smiled and said, "No mommy it's fun to spin!" I was completely and totally perplexed. The spinning did seem to be enjoyable to him and I didn't ask him to stop. When he wanted to spin I let him.

By this time my son was able to take a shower, with my assistance, as he was only three years old. While helping him shower he would scream as if the water touching his skin were needles going through his skin. He would scream and cry uncontrollably. I would immediately check the temperature of the water making sure it was neither too hot nor too cold. I was certain the water was just the right temperature. I would wash them as quickly as I could while he cried and screamed. After each shower, I would have to swaddle him in a large bath towel as tightly as I could and sit with him and rock him in a rocking chair as if he were an infant.

Around that same time, I can remember my son running and crashing into trees at top speed. These were not young sapling trees but full-grown oak trees. Each time he hit a tree I would catch up to him to see if he was ok. Each time he was just laughing and running to the next tree. He was clearly enjoying himself. I was extremely perplexed by this behavior. I couldn't understand how crashing into trees at top speed pleasurable, fun was and felt good while taking a nice warm shower was painful and felt bad.

My son was also extremely hyper. When he was awake he was running. He was either running constantly or he was asleep. There was no sitting quietly drawing pictures in coloring books are doing puzzles. This was a time before iPads. He could watch TV, but if the TV was off he was running or sleeping. The other thing he was doing at this time was talking constantly. He would talk or sleep there was no just sitting quietly playing or listening. When he was doing anything he was talking constantly. During the days his pattern was run, talk nap and repeat. There was no in between it was either go go or completely off.

Middle

Around this time I got a new job at a sensory integration clinic. They were looking for a speech therapist that could run a new program that was going to start at the clinic. One of the requirements of this job was to read a book called the Out of Sync Child by Carol Stockman. I got to about page 5 or six of the book and I realize that my son was in this book. I read as much of that book as I could on the day I got it. The very next day I went into work and said, "My son needs to come in for an evaluation."

I brought my son in and he was diagnosed with sensory integration dysfunction. I had never heard of anything like this before. I was assured that this condition was treatable. He also required listening therapy to reduce the need to speak all the time. It should also calm him down enough so that he would be able to sit quietly and learn. I was ecstatic!

I was told that my son needed to be on a brushing program. He would need to have his entire body brushed from head to toe five times a day, every single day. This treatment needed to be followed up by joint compressions to every joint in his body. This treatment would take 10 to 15 minutes, but it had to be done five times a day. I said, "Well that is not something I cannot do. I work here every day and my son is in school every day. I can't do this brushing." They said, "You have to find people in his world who will be onboard to complete this brushing program on a daily basis. You're going to have to train everybody in your son's world to do this brushing program if you want him to recover. Without this, he's not going to normalize his sense of touch or his vestibular system. He's not going to be able to sit down to attend and learn all the things that he needs to learn if this treatment is not implemented. It has to be done five times a day that's the only way for it to be effective." Wow! I thought to myself how am I going to do this how am I going to get everyone in my son's world on board with this brushing program?

At the time my son was attending a private preschool. I decided to put him into the same private school where my older son was attending. I also wanted him to be in private school because I was afraid he was going to be labeled as a special education. As an educator from a family of educators, I was worried about the stigma that would be placed on my child if he was labeled a special-education student. For that reason and I placed my sons in private school. I thought I would have a little bit more power if my son was in private school.

Now, I was faced with the task of training everyone in my son's world on his brushing program. I knew that it was very important to let everyone know who my son was and what the recent evaluations had discovered. I decided to call a meeting of my son's teachers but not just the classroom teacher I also invited the gym teacher, the art teacher, the school nurse, the headmaster and the assistant headmaster. It was important for me to have school administrators at the meeting. I knew that they would be able to ensure that the teachers would follow through on what I was going to share about my son. I couldn't just stop at the level of the teacher. I needed to make sure that administrators knew what I was doing. They could provide a directive to members of the educational staff. I invited specific members of my son's educational team because they each had a specific role.

I needed the school nurse to be present because, the school nurses are usually most comfortable dealing with a child's body. I would let her be in charge of this brushing program. I needed to have the gym teacher there because the gym teacher usually is someone who understands the physicality is of a child's body. I knew that they were going to be times when my son would need to go to the gym to run off some energy before he was asked to sit down and write his name. I knew that they were going to be times when he would need to be in the gym when it wasn't necessarily gym time. I knew that I needed to have a headmaster at present. The headmaster would allow the gym teacher to let my son run in the gym when he needed to.

That first meeting with my son's educational team went very well. The entire team thanked me for explaining who my son was to them. They were happy to have a better understanding of how they could help him. They also stated that the information that I had shared would help other children in that school. I was empowered by the success of that meeting. I was empowered by being able to shed greater light and understanding and who my son was and what he needed in order to be his best self. I was empowered by the respect that I received from the team. I was empowered by how they respected me as the authority of my son. I was empowered by how they receive the information and share that it would help other children who were also exhibiting similar but not as severe behaviors.

My son had a successful pre-K year in that school. The next year he went to Kindergarten in a different school. It was still a private school but it was a bit more affordable for my family. I had a whole new team that I needed to train. I invited the entire team again and explained who my son had been and the treatment that he needed to receive. The new team implemented the treatment as well.

During the summertime, I also trained every camp counselor and every camp director on how to complete the brushing program and the joint compressions. I have course encountered some people especially during the summer that did not want to participate in the brushing program. Summer camp is not educational so of course, camp directors and camp counselors just wanted to participate in summer activities. But I knew that the brushing program along with the joint compressions had to continue throughout the summer months. So when I encounter people that did not want to participate in the program I just moved onto the person who was willing to participate in the program.

My son was on a brushing program for 18 months. He was brushed five times a day every day for 18 months. Either by myself, his father, or another person in his world. At the end of the 18 months brushing my son was able to have a normal response to water hitting his skin in the shower. He no longer ran into trees. However, he did continue to spin however. By this time he is seven years old. He is now in a public school.

By this time he was in first grade, I sent my son to a public school because I wasn't sure that the private school could offer him all the services at a public school could offer him. I also could no longer afford the tuition of the private school. So my son went to public school. That was a huge change. We now had much larger classroom sizes many more students in the classroom and less teachers in the classroom that was the biggest shock. In first grade, there were 20-25 children in my son's class. He had a difficult time navigating all the things that he needs to remember in a public school setting. He would often forget to grab his lunch box before into the cafeteria. In a small private school, this was not such a big issue because the kids sat and ate lunch in their classroom. However, in a public school in the cafeteria was on the other side of the building. Any first grader that forgot their lunch box created a bigger issue. How would we get the lunchbox out of the classroom?

Once in public school, the teachers in this environment were more accustomed to recognizing differences in children. I can remember after the first day of first grade the teacher called me to say your son is different and we are recommending him for testing. First, we will ensemble a child study team. Essentially this was a meeting of school officials including the psychologist, the principal, a teacher, a special education teacher, and parents. This team was gathered to determine why a child might be behaving in a certain way. I was excited to go to the child study team I had already trained two or three teams by this time and all I had to do was update my son's history. I had been keeping an anecdotal history on my son for six years. All I needed to do was to make fresh copies.

When I got to the child study team meeting I handed out those documents. I started the meeting by saying, "This is who my son has been over the past six years. This is where we were, this is what we did, and this is where we are now.

In that meeting, I also stated that I was a speech therapist in a public school. I had a clear understanding of the special education process. I had also contacted my own IEP meetings for children who had different needs. I wanted the team to be aware that I was familiar with the entire process.

My son was able to stay in regular education for all of the first grade. However, at the beginning of second grade, the team recommended that he go through educational testing. He would undergo a test for my school psychologist. He was also screened by a speech language pathologist. This was actually a very good thing because my son was having difficulty learning how to read he was reversing letters and numbers he and he was extremely frustrated. By the middle of second grade, he was finally identified with a specific special educational need. He was now allowed to participate in a learning support classroom. Within the first week of attending his new class, I could tell that he was beginning to relax. The first day he got homework from his learning support teacher he actually smiled and said, "This is so easy!" Before that, he would really struggle with the homework that his second grade teacher was giving him. Let's talk about homework.

For my second do your homework every night he would have to spin on an office chair for 10 to 15 minutes every single night. I can remember a time when he unscrewed the chair. The screws actually dropped out of the chair and landed on the floor because he was spinning at such a rapid of speed. I also had a small trampoline at the time. He had to jump for another 10 minutes after spinning before he could sit down to do any homework. This was what we did on a nightly basis in order to complete any homework. My son needed to spin and jump regularly throughout all of the second grade and third grade. By fourth grade, he no longer needed that sensory input by this time he was ten. He still needed to have the support of an IEP for remembering information, spelling, and all of his language arts.

End

That IEP stayed in place until my son was in 11th grade. When he got to 11th grade his special-education team contacted me and said your son no longer needs special instruction. I remember getting that phone call. I remember being completely and totally shocked. He was 18 years old at the time and he had been receiving services since he was 18 months old. I had trained every single team from 18 months old all the way to 18 years old. Here I was being told that my hard work had paid off and that my son no longer qualified to receive these services.

Needless to say, I was extremely concerned and because I knew my rights I asked for a 504 plan. A 504 plan is still under the Americans with Disabilities Act and it still allowed my son to have some accommodations throughout 12th grade.

Final thoughts

At the time of this writing, my son has just graduated from high school. He graduated as an A and B student. During his 12 grade year, he participated in all of the senior activities. He went to the prom he worked on the school play as a stage crew member. He has a large group of friends. His grades were so strong that he was able to receive a partial scholarship to a small university. He plans to live on campus. He is also able to drive. No one would ever know looking at my son today at 19 the challenges that he had as a young person. He doesn't resemble that individual in any shape or form. He has achieved a complete and total recovery. No one would ever know that he had received services for 16 years. I am completely and totally proud of everything that he has achieved. I know that he has worked very hard and I am extremely proud of him. I also know that part of his success is due how I fight for him in those early days. Fighting for him in the early days and stay focused on the ultimate goal helped him to be the successful individual that he is now.

Confession #14 The Journey to "Light Your Way"
Irina Kapelyan

My name is Irina Kapelyan. I am 38 years of age. My parents Boris and Inna along with my brother Alexander and I immigrated to the United States from Rechitsa, Belarus Russia in 1990. We relocated to Chicago from the former Soviet Union when I was 10 years old for a better life and the opportunity for me and my younger brother to strive for the American Dream. I grew up with the same intentions in the back of my mind, wanting the same for my family to create a better future. Working for what my parents had wanted so much for me, I did what most people who are successful do. I went to college, got my Bachelors Degree in Human Resources and went back for my Masters in Business Administration. I worked as the Human Resources Manager in the corporate world. "Living the Dream" though I felt unfulfilled. I always worked very hard only to accomplish what seemed like it was making someone else's dreams come true. My son Benjamin was being raised half a day at a Russian daycare.

In 2008, My Twin flame Jason came into my life, which the fire of our love has never flickered or faded in the 9 years we have spent together. Combined we have three children and our youngest child Grace we had together. Jason's son Drake is 16, Benjamin is 12, and

Grace is 7 years old. Jason and our children are everything that I am and they are number one to me!

I'm known around our house as simply "Mom", as the norm in our house we often hear from across the room the kids dropping "Mom Bombs" which are yells at the top of their lungs for me to swoop into action. Often, it's Grace with her stuffed elephant she received when she was born at the hospital that she cannot be without even at 7 years old. She shows she cares for something other than herself and these are signs of a wonderful mother in the making so we enjoy the searches   for "Ele" while we can because she is growing up so fast.

I have always strived to spend as much time as I can with my children and our families. We have so many family members and we are all very close and keep in touch daily with my cousins, aunts, uncles, nieces, and nephews.

I often felt like I was a one woman show, featuring a balancing act, juggling the demands of work and being a mother, I wanted something more. I wanted to spend my time raising my children was how I deeply felt.

I came to a realization that this job wasn't the dream I wanted and knew that I needed a different way so I can be the one to raise my children with my values, morals, and ethics.

Always knowing that one day I would be a mother, it really mattered that I was able to be there and take care of my newborn for as long as I could. On Aug 7, 2005, I was in the hospital and gave birth to Benjamin. I spent the next four days in the hospital with forty stitches taking several months to recover. I couldn't be happier while being home with Benjamin for two months and went to college at night which went against all my instincts which urged me to be with him. During that time Benjamin was approaching six months old as I was finishing up the last semester of college and graduated with my Bachelor's in Human Resources degree. It was quite challenging because I nursed Benjamin, and always felt torn when I was away. Ben suffered with pretty bad GERD, and would constantly spit up and wanted me for comfort. I had to be very careful about our nutrition since it had a big effect on baby Benjamin and ensured he was only fed organic food. I was very committed to being the best Mom I could be. I knew that my ex husband wanted me to finish my college degree and it was important to him that I did. I was fortunate enough to stay home with Ben until he was around 15 months when I returned to work again.

I didn't agree with my ex husband about returning to work, "but you have a degree" was a strong case in point. It just didn't make sense for me to pay almost two thirds of my salary to have someone else spend time with my child. Just think about all of the first moments that I would miss and the close bond I may lose if I am not a part of that experience for Benjamin. I wanted to be there for ALL of that.

Not with much enthusiasm, I went back to work as a Human Resources Manager. It was very difficult to balance a stressful workload, being a new mom and being back in school yet again for my MBA. I was going with the flow and through the motions of living "The American Dream"... Go back to school, work, work, and also work hard for someone else while being torn apart inside about not being able to stay home with my child.

My marriage was taking a toll me and speaking my mind was not received very well by my ex. It was more of a dictatorship than a relationship. When Ben was three years old our divorce was being filed. It was a very tough decision to make and none of my family supported me, but I knew in my heart it was for the best for me and Benjamin. I decided to follow my gut feeling, and leave almost 10 years of my life behind with a three year old and start over again.

At the time I was working at a Veterinary Research Company in HR. I felt my job was secure so Benjamin and I will be OK, or so I thought. Fortunately and also, unfortunately, my boss at the time decided to sell part of his company and merge with the IT Company they had been outsourcing. The economy took a bad turn and that is when chaos emerged. Lots of changes were being made in our company and I was the bearer of bad news to inform employee layoffs and their benefits were being taken away.

I was done with "love" for anyone else besides my son and myself. I stayed focused on work, my education and being with my son. I would go to the gym to strengthen my body, mind, and soul. However, I will never forget the day, when a message popped up on my computer screen and it said: "Putting in an order for supplements and protein, anyone let me know what you need". The message was from Jason the IT guy. Jason originally was outsourced by my boss for IT services through the company he worked for, now worked for "our boss" doing Network Administration and Consulting.

Prior to the merger, Jason and I saw each other in passing briefly, but never really had any meaningful time to talk. I got to know him a bit more when the companies merged and learned that he was an MMA fighter and also was very passionate about Brazilian Jiu Jitsu. Because I had been overweight most my life and being on my own health journey, one which my ex husband could never understand, I was into fitness as well. Jason also was going through personal issues with his ex and son Drake who lived with his mother in Georgia. We both found comfort in going to the gym to lift weights and also train in Jiu Jitsu together. Despite all the drama in our lives before each other, we became good friends and relied on each other's support. We have similar interests in being our healthiest, and Jiu Jitsu is a great way to stay healthy and learn some amazing skills.

Our friendship grew even stronger when I got the news that papers were final and I finally was able to move out of my house where I resided with my ex and Benjamin. I was looking for a place so was he, so we decided to move in together. Benjamin loved being with Jason, even though Ben didn't speak a word of English at the time and their communication was limited. My ex only wanted for us to speak to Ben only in Russian. Jason and Benjamin still were able to form a bond as Jason also was a coach/mentor figure to him. Benjamin was starting to learn English and had a bad lisp, all his "L" sounds were sounding like "W," but with some practice and help of Jason, Ben was able to correct that. Even though we were both going through a lot in our lives, Jason and I had remained strong by going to the gym and taking care of our mind, body, and soul and of course just being there for each other always.

Everything was going well for about six months, we had our jobs, our apartment, and we had our new routine, and loved spending time with each other. Until one day, we got a letter from the upper management that our company was downsizing and hours were getting cut at work. That was almost expected from the new management with new rules and policies and of course layoffs. At the time we were both facing being laid-off and pretty shaken up not knowing what our futures will be.

The idea of being small business owners was something I never thought I would be, but we both wanted to spend more time together doing more of what makes us happy. We searched for the best business that we could own and simply free up our time and be less necessary to be there while our business was operational. We decided to buy Duds 'n Suds Laundromat & Dry Clean in Rolling Meadows, IL. I was going to be my own boss, work my own hours, spend more time with my son and also to our surprise we were expecting a baby girl, Grace!

Jason was helping me run the business and raise our two kids Grace and Ben and we had Drake fly in every school break and summer as he lived with his mother in Georgia since he was seven years old. We hired Jason's mom to work as a laundry attendant and inherited another attendant and without her, we wouldn't know what we were doing, Patricia had worked at this Laundromat for seven years prior to us taking over. We understood Patty's worry that we would fire her and we told her our story and that we were giving her a raise and she would never be fired when we sat her down to talk she let out all her emotions and really was panicked about her job. Patty was originally from Chile, South America and she primarily spoke only Spanish with very little English. We knew she was dependable and hardworking and deserved that raise saying for many years never having a raise. Patty went to night school on her nights off and learned officially how to read, write and speak English and we helped a lot with that too. I can relate to not knowing the language as

I came here in 1990 we did not know any English. Back to Patty, we immediately gave her a raise and paid both of our employees well and gave them more time off and gave bonuses and gifts for every occasion. Jason and I did everything side by side and it was such a great business, we were booming and growing as our children too was there with us. Having the time freedom, we trained in Jiu Jitsu a lot and Jason was able to pursue his professional career in MMA and winning at Bellator 75, and I was living my dream of being able to be with my kids.

We were able to afford a new home and moved closer to Duds 'n Suds and bought a new SUV and got a full body wrap that had pink bubbles all over it with our logo. We got a lot of attention when we would be driving our car to do pickup and delivery of supplies or delivery customers' laundry and dry cleaned clothes. We had grown this part of the business from zero customers to well over 300 customers by advertising and reaching out to businesses for their linen and outsourced dry cleaning services they charge an arm and a leg for at a hotel that we do business within the area. Jason and I were building a tower for it all to crumble to dust.

After one and a half great years where we reinvested into new machines, and a complete overhaul of this large Laundromat. We added 8 flat screen TV's, Italian leather couches and modern chairs and tables. We had video games and it was just a fun place to do laundry. The large apartment complexes behind Duds were sold and housed many of our regular walk up customers. We were smart and built a delivery service that kept us afloat. Little by little we were sinking though. We had to pay for the loans we had so we were trying to sell the business. We had a lot of potential buyers but it never sold. We would eventually bite the bullet and sell the equipment and scrap the whole place.

After five years we were broke and now we couldn't afford our rent at our townhouse. We ended up losing our home and our business. We were down but never out. We moved most of our belongings of a 3000 square foot home into a storage facility and in order to save money, we would occasionally move from one storage facility to another.

We started buying storage units like on TV and started an online business plus we set up shop at Wolff's flea market selling tools where we employed Jason's brother Dan to operate part of the time.

We were approached about The Ambit Opportunity at about the time all this was going on and we went to a presentation at night and I was intrigued but Jason and I couldn't justify spending any money on investing in ourselves on yet another one of my brilliant ideas and it looked too good to be true. So we said maybe, and we left after explaining how it all sounds well and good by us we just don't have time and our finances are out of order.

We ended up partnering with a Jiu Jitsu and MMA gym and Jason also worked between boxing clubs teaching cardio boxing and PT's on the side. This gym allowed us to have our own business by splitting half of our client's payments made. We had a full class every other night and we got to do Jiu Jitsu since Jason was the kid's teacher as well. We also cleaned the gym and ended up teaching more for less and it got the best of everyone and what we loved became a labor of love but it didn't pay the bills in this location and we planned to move. We were in agreement with the Gym Owners to open a location with more capacity and in a highly visible location. We were given the runaround and soon parted ways with the gym and the owners.

So we did what we had to do and I got a job at the bank and Jason provided care for the kids while he was still looking for work back in the IT field.

At the bank, I would be in one location one day and another the next plus multiple senior homes to operate onsite banks for the elderly. I opened more accounts than anyone at any location by far just by talking to people and providing solutions that fit their needs. The pay was not as high but I only took this position in order to stop the financial bleeding we were hemorrhaging and it was close to home and the kids.

I took a new position at a company that I met an owner who was a customer at the bank I worked at. I was offered to begin learning the business as a customer service representative and then be gradually moved into Human Resources in time. Little to my surprise I was kept in the windowless cold area answering customer calls and I was so well liked in this position they wanted to keep me there at the salary I was originally told would increase but I had seen enough to know that I was being used for less than I was worth. Jason's son Drake was visiting for the summer and he wanted to stay and live with us full time and I needed to handle all the paperwork and school transfers and requested time to do this and they looked me in the eyes and said: "Your children are not our problem." I quit on the spot and had the reassurance from Jason who also worked there for a time being was working at another company making a lot more money than me and either he or I were going to have to take care of this, so I sacrificed and left.

My parents and I bought a house and remodeled it to accommodate both of our families and we are living with them together. As my father is aging he needs a caregiver and I am home with him and my kids as a caregiver part time.

Jason ended up hurting his back at work lifting super heavy batteries for servers. He was working and had to move many of these all weeks leading up to an accident on the job. He to this day cannot lift anything heavy. He requires a surgery and the employer is denying the claim. We had a lawyer and was waiting for a hearing and it has almost been a year now.

So now he and I had no job, besides a part time caregiver for my father whom all money goes straight into the mortgage and bills. We have two really nice 2016 cars a Camaro and a Cruze. Income ceases just when everything was going great.

I had been interviewing since leaving my job, but I decided to not settle for less than my degree and my value in experience. One day I saw on Facebook a post regarding an income opportunity happening nearby. I was interested so I asked for more info. I went to the presentation Jason stayed with the kids at home and when I returned I was so excited! I knew this was the way we would turn it all around. Not quickly, but over time. Financial freedom is having enough that your bills are paid and you can do what you want wherever you want to be.

Jason and I formed a corporation and called it Light Your Way Inc. and are Senior Consultants now with Ambit Energy. I feel that this is the greatest business and company I have ever been a part of. I can work on the beach or anywhere in the world meanwhile help others to have these choices in their lives. I can spend time with my family and help make our dreams a reality. Recently Jason, the kids and I went to Dallas Texas to our annual event Ambition, where we gather to train with each other and celebrate everyone's success.

After all the trials and misfortunes Jason and I always stood strong and never gave up on our dreams of being business owners and being able to have the flexibility and time freedom to pursue our dreams and passions in helping others as well as being with our family as much as possible.

Want to write your own book?
Don't want to make the same mistakes we did? Keep reading...

Turning your story and your experience into a book, might just be the single most important decision you make today. You have been shaped by your experiences. What problems, hurts, pains, and trials have been through and what did you learn from them?

Your book, your story will most likely come from your greatest hurt. You must understand the very experiences that you regretted, resented most in life, the ones that you want to hide and forget <u>are the very experiences we need right now.</u>

You must be willing to share them, have to stop covering them up and honestly admit your faults, failures and fears. People are always more encouraged when we share how Gods grace helped us in our weakness than brag about how great we are."

My goal for you is that you write your story and become an author without the costly mistakes and headaches of traditional publishing.

Save yourself from the same mistakes we made, saving you time, frustration and a lot of money. There is a better way and we have it in a 4 part video course delivered to you each week by email. Here is what you get each week:

Video 1/Week 1: Position Where to start to write your own book.
-Identify how much you have overcome and how important it is to share your story to help others.
-How to identify your story, what your story really cost you and how to place a real dollar value on your experience.
-How to determine who your audience is and how much your story is worth to them.
-The 3 steps to developing your story and how to look differently at that "negative experience" you have been through.

Video 2/Week 2: Publish
-Why you do not need a publisher and why a publisher will probably not talk to you anyways.
-Why you need to be an author to stand out, get noticed, and be remembered.
-4 steps to package your story so others can very quickly relate to you and take away the lesson from your painful "negative" experience.

-The #1 resource you must know for designing digital and/or print marketing.

Video 3/ Week 3: Promise
-Discover everything I wish I knew before writing and publishing my 1st book.
-The easy way and the hard way to publishing your 1st book.
-Why you do not need to buy boxes or books and make exhausting trips to the post office
-How much money you can really expect to make from your book and where the money really is in being an author.

Video 4/Week 4: Promote
-How to get your book or product on Amazon.com
-Why selling your book on Amazon is a terrible strategy.
-How to turn your physical book into a #1 Best Seller.
-What is a sales funnel and why you must consider using a funnel to generate more revenue from a book sale.
-Why writing your book is one thing and selling your book is another. And if you hate selling I am going to share with you a strategy on how you never have to sell your book.

If All This Did Was...

Support you in writing out and placing a real dollar value on your experiences. Would it be worth it?

If all this did was separate yourself from all the other mom's who just judge and criticize others mom's accomplishments. Would it be worth it?

If all this did was get you invited to be a part of new & fun opportunities? Would it be worth it?

If all this did was get you at least 3 new opportunities or clients over the next 3 months. Would it be worth it?

If all this did was save you the 3-5 years of wasted time & energy trying to figure this stuff out on your own. Would it be worth it?

4 Week Video Course
Special Offer From the Author
One Payment of $119 Was $197 or 3 Payments of $49
To register email info@fulltimemom.org

Want to be a featured author in our next book?

"How To Write, Publish & Market a #1 Best Selling Book in the next 12 months"

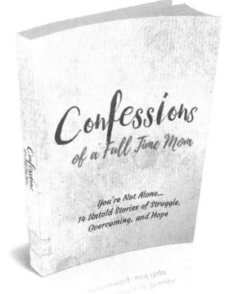

Here Is The Deal:
You only have to write 2500 words.
It is a 12 month commitment.
We only have 15 spots available.

The Investment:
One Payment ~~$595~~ Now $495
or 2 Payments $297

Here's What To Do Next
To apply with payment go to: www.FullTimeMom.org/apply

For more information go to: www.FullTimeMom.org/book

33240729R00066

Made in the USA
Middletown, DE
12 January 2019